CHE GUEVARA

YOU WIN OR YOU DIE

STUART A. KALLEN

TWENTY-FIRST CENTURY BOOKS / MINNEAPOLIS

12/7/2012

Twenty-First Century Books
A division of Lerner Publishing Group, Inc.
241 First Avenue North
Minneapolis, MN 55401 U.S.A.

Website address: www.lernerbooks.com

Library of Congress Cataloging-in-Publication Data

Kallen, Stuart A., 1955–
    Che Guevara : you win or you die / by Stuart A. Kallen.
        p.   cm.
    Includes bibliographical references and index.
    ISBN: 978-0-8225-9035-4 (lib. bdg. : alk. paper)
    1. Guevara, Ernesto, 1928–1967—Juvenile literature. 2. Guerrillas—Latin
America—Biography—Juvenile literature. 3. Revolutionaries—Cuba—Biography—
Juvenile literature. 4. Cuba—History—1959–1990—Juvenile literature. 5. Latin
America—History—1948–1980—Juvenile literature. I. Title.
F2849.22.G85K36 2013
980.03'5092—dc23 [B]   2011045480

Manufactured in the United States of America
1 – BP – 7/15/12

CONTENTS

SHOTS HEARD ROUND THE WORLD

Bolivia Confirms Guevara's Death; Body Displayed.

—*New York Times*, October 10, 1967

On October 9, 1967, a drunken Bolivian army sergeant, Mario Terán, walked into a mud-walled schoolhouse in a tiny village in Bolivia. Inside, he found a wounded man, Ernesto "Che" Guevara. "I know you've come to kill me," said Guevara. "Shoot, coward!"

Terán raised his semiautomatic rifle and shot nine times. Che Guevara was dead.

Mario Terán was not a hired assassin. He had not spent weeks or even days planning Guevara's execution. He was just an ordinary soldier who volunteered to shoot a prisoner, carrying out orders given by the Bolivian president. While Terán might not have cared much whether Che Guevara lived or died, many other, more powerful people cared very deeply about Guevara's fate.

CREAR DOS, TRES... MUCHOS VIET NAM, ES LA CONSIGNA

CHE EN BOLIVIA

Che Guevara had been a hero of the Cuban Revolution of the 1950s. ABOVE: *a Cuban newspaper reports on his death in 1967.* OPPOSITE: *A famous portrait of Guevara is still recognized around the world.*

Fidel Castro (left), the leader of Cuba since 1959, poses with Che Guevara in 1960. Many people hoped that the two men would bring economic fairness and justice to Cuba.

A native of Argentina, Che Guevara had become famous around the globe as the handsome face and fiery voice of revolution. In the late 1950s, he had fought alongside another magnetic revolutionary—Fidel Castro—to successfully overthrow the much hated Fulgencio Batista, a corrupt and brutal Cuban dictator.

In Cuba, an island nation in the Caribbean Sea, not far from the United States, Guevara and Castro struck a blow not only against Batista and his government. They also declared war on capitalism, an economic system based on private property and individual wealth. The revolutionaries decried capitalism as a corrupt system. They believed it put too much power in the hands of a few wealthy individuals and big businesses. They said it exploited poor farmers and other workers. After taking over in Cuba, Guevara and Castro stripped many wealthy people and companies of their land and power. They set up systems designed to spread wealth and resources among ordinary workers.

After the Cuban Revolution, Guevara hoped to lead similar revolutions in other parts of the world. But his revolutionary goals earned him many enemies. Big businesses saw him as a threat to their power. The U.S. government, which had close ties to big businesses, saw him as a threat to its power. Dictators around the world, many of whom had the backing of big business and the U.S. government, saw him as a threat to their power. So when Che Guevara was assassinated in Bolivia, many powerful people cheered.

But many others mourned. Guevara's message of economic justice appealed to millions of poor people throughout the world. Many intellectuals, students, and political activists also saw Guevara as a hero. Nine days after the assassination, more than one million Cubans gathered in the Plaza de la Revolución, in the Cuban capital of Havana, to honor the fallen revolutionary. It soon became apparent that by killing Guevara, the Bolivian army had created a martyr—a hero to the cause of revolution.

It's no surprise that Che Guevara captured the adoration of millions. He was a dashing radical fighting for freedom and equality. His powerful enemies viewed him as a dangerous threat. The events leading to his assassination are surrounded with suspense, mystery, and action. History has shown Guevara's murder to be one of the central stories of the 1960s, a decade marked by rebellion, hope, and change.

CHAPTER ONE

THE MAKING OF A REBEL

> I feel my nostrils dilated, tasting the acrid smell of gunpowder and of blood, of [the] dead enemy; now my body contorts, ready for the fight, and I prepare my being...so that in it the bestial howling of the triumphant [people] can resonate with new vibrations and hopes.
>
> —Che Guevara, 1954, after witnessing the CIA-led coup in Guatemala

Ernesto "Che" Guevara Lynch Jr. was born in Rosario, Argentina, on June 14, 1928. His father, Ernesto Guevara Lynch Sr., had a degree in architecture and engineering and invested in a number of farming and business enterprises.

Ernesto's mother, Celia de la Serna, was of noble South American lineage. One of her ancestors had been a royal viceroy—a representative of the Spanish king—in Peru. Another had been a famous general in Argentina. Celia's father had been a wealthy ambassador and congressman in Argentina. Celia inherited a large sum of money from her father the year after Ernesto was born.

If Celia's ancestors signified traditional political power, her husband's relatives represented revolution and adventure. Grandparents on both sides of Ernesto Sr.'s family were forced to leave Argentina to escape repression during the dictatorship of General Juan Manuel de Rosas (1829–1852). One family member went to California in the mid-1800s, fought off American Indian attacks, and struggled unsuccessfully as a gold miner. Another earned a fortune in San Francisco, California, before returning to Argentina. Commenting on his family, Guevara Sr. wrote, "They were all political exiles [people who must leave their country]. This must have influenced Ernesto as a child, as he heard talk of my grandparents, who in their youth had to leave their homes and earn their living in a foreign country."

OPPOSITE: *Ernesto Guevara stands outside his family home in Argentina around 1934.*

A CURSED ILLNESS

When Ernesto was around three years old, he was stricken with asthma, a disease of the lungs. Ernesto's asthma was one of the worst cases his doctors had ever seen. In an era before inhalers and other modern medicines, the boy hiccuped, coughed, and gasped for breath for days at a time. The family consulted dozens of doctors and tried a wide array of unsuccessful cures to find relief for their son. Doctors believed that the heat and humidity of Buenos Aires, where the family was living, worsened Ernesto's asthma. The family moved several times, trying to find a region where Ernesto could live in better health. As Guevara Sr. described it, "Ernesto's asthma was shaping all our decisions. Each day brought a new restriction to our freedom of movement and we were at the mercy of his cursed illness."

> ## "We were at the mercy of his cursed illness."
> —Ernesto Guevara Sr.

In 1932 the Guevara family, which by then included Ernesto's younger brother and sister, moved to Córdoba, about 350 miles (563 kilometers) north of Buenos Aires. Córdoba is at the foot of the Sierras Chicas mountain range. Doctors recommended it because the dry mountain climate was thought to be helpful for asthmatics. Ernesto's condition did improve, although he still was occasionally bedridden with asthma attacks.

The Guevara family thrived in Córdoba. Guevara Sr. earned a good living managing the construction of a golf course at the Sierra Hotel, the city's most prestigious resort. In between asthma attacks, Ernesto swam, ran, and played rugby with enthusiasm. In his teen years, Ernesto performed extreme antics that earned him the nickname El Loco, meaning "crazy person" or "madman." He was a daredevil with no fear—and little sense. For example, Ernesto performed a tightrope act for his friends, crossing a deep ravine on a metal pipe. He jumped from high rock ledges into rivers and rode his bicycle over long railroad bridges, despite the risk of oncoming trains.

MISERY AND INJUSTICE

The Sierra Hotel attracted Argentina's upper classes. Through his job at the hotel, Guevara Sr. was able to introduce his son to powerful politicians, military officers, and wealthy landowners.

The rich hotel guests stood apart from the majority of the Córdoba population. The city's working classes lived in extreme poverty, residing in rough shanties (slum houses) built on hillsides and in ravines. Unemployment was rampant. Those who did work struggled to make a living from farming, labored in dangerous mines, or performed backbreaking work in marble and limestone quarries. If workers protested or went on strike (refused to work until management made improvements), bosses sent company security guards to beat them or called the police to arrest them. The children of the working poor

In this photograph, Ernesto is around twelve years old.

POVERTY IN ARGENTINA

Che Guevara's wealthy family lived in a beautiful resort town populated by tourists and rich Argentineans. However, the majority of residents in the region lived in extreme poverty. Ernesto Guevara Sr. described the circumstance of the working people:

The children of these workers were . . . malnourished, badly dressed, in poor health and did not attend school regularly. The working class was exploited. . . . They ate little, their housing was appalling, they worked more hours than the law permitted . . . they carried out [unsafe] jobs without the proper level of compensation [pay]. At the time there were no laws to protect the workers and they, in turn, felt cornered. . . .

Many of the children did not attend school for lack of adequate clothing. Many school-age children worked as shoeshine boys, or sold fruit, eggs, or [snacks], or hung around the [railway] station terminals and bus stops or places frequented by tourists to beg for a coin. These children developed an instinct for survival, they used their imagination and became quick at grabbing whatever they could lay their hands on. Many of them became petty thieves.

Normally messy, Ernesto dressed in a suit and tie for this photograph, taken around 1950.

were malnourished, dressed in rags, and received little or no medical care. Their families could not afford to send them to school. Many young people begged in the streets or turned to crime to pay for food.

In Argentina only about two hundred powerful families controlled most of the nation's wealth. Ernesto was keenly aware of the gap between rich and poor. He had a few friends among the upper classes, but most of his friends were the sons and daughters of low-wage laborers who worked at the hotel as caddies, waiters, maids, and cooks.

One of Ernesto's friends lived with his parents and five brothers and sisters in a tiny one-room shack. The eight members of the family had only one bed to sleep in and used rags and old newspapers for covers. According to Guevara Sr.,

> [Ernesto] had the opportunity of living among the destitute [poor] as well as among the wealthy, and he drew a lesson from it that he never forgot. . . . [He] learned from his friends what real misery is and was able to appreciate the injustices to which they were subjected by the official institutions that relegated [assigned] them to a life of poverty.

HELPING **HUMANITY**

The Guevara home was filled with more than three thousand books, and Ernesto was passionate about poetry. When sick in bed with asthma, he read and memorized verses by American poet Walt Whitman, British poets John Keats and Rudyard Kipling, and the renowned Chilean poet Pablo Neruda. As Ernesto grew older, he developed diverse tastes and devoured books on philosophy, psychology, engineering, mathematics, economics, politics, history, and religion. When he came across concepts that spoke to him, he wrote them down in his journals.

By the time he was seventeen, Ernesto had developed into an intelligent, attractive young man. He was slim with wide shoulders, penetrating brown eyes, and pale skin. Many young women took an interest in Ernesto, and he enjoyed reciting poetry to them. As his friend Miriam Urrutia later recalled, "The truth is, we were all a little in love with Ernesto."

In 1947 Ernesto left several girlfriends behind when he entered the University of Buenos Aires. Years later, he explained his decision to study medicine there: "I dreamed of being a famous researcher, of working tirelessly to discover something which could eventually be made available to the whole of humanity."

Ernesto was a good student. He studied medicine for three years while working part-time at an allergy research clinic. Young men in Argentina were required to serve one year in the army, but Ernesto was exempt because of his chronic asthma. He was glad not to have to do military service. He told his friends, "These [horrible] lungs have been useful for a change."

CHE "THE PIG" GUEVARA

When Che Guevara was a college student, his indifference to fashion and good hygiene was legendary. He often bragged about not washing his clothes. His main fashion statement was a white shirt he called "the weekly"—that's how often he washed it. And by washing, he meant wearing it in the bathtub. Guevara never wore a tie. His footwear consisted of old boots—sometimes an unmatched set. Guevara loved the attention his lack of style and cleanliness brought him. He delighted in a nickname given to him by his colleagues: El Chancho (the Pig). Despite his dirty clothing, women were still fascinated by Guevara's good looks. He had affairs with women in all walks of life, including his parents' housekeeper, prostitutes, revolutionaries, and the daughters of aristocrats.

Guevara (left) shares a laugh with Alberto Granado (center) and another friend. Guevara and Granado took a long tour of South America in 1952.

TWO TRAMPS **ON THE ROAD**

By 1952 Guevara was tired of his life as a student. He wanted to travel, so on January 4, he set off with a friend, Alberto Granado, on a 5,000-mile (8,000 km) trip on a 1939 Norton motorcycle. Guevara kept a detailed journal during the eight-month adventure through Argentina, Chile, Peru, Colombia, and Venezuela. The motorcycle broke down after a few months, so the pair was forced to hitch rides. As Guevara wrote in his diary, he and Granado were just "two tramps with packs on our backs, and the grime of the road encrusted in our overalls, shadows of our former aristocratic ways."

As a tramp on the road, Guevara spoke to many people who lived in grinding poverty. In Chuquicamata, Chile, in March 1952, he met an impoverished elderly couple. They were members of Chile's Communist Party. This party wished to change Chile from a capitalist society into a Communist one. In a Communist system, the government controls the means of production—farms, factories, and other businesses that produce wealth. The products from these businesses are supposed to be distributed

Guevara and Granado set out from Argentina on a motorcycle in 1952. After the bike broke down, the two men hitchhiked through South America.

equally among all the people in society. This theory of economic fairness and justice appealed to Guevara.

The elderly couple told Guevara how the Anaconda Copper Mining Company, a U.S.-based corporation (big, privately owned business), exploited workers at the Chuquicamata mine. The miners and their families lived in dismal poverty, with little medical care. The local cemetery was filled with workers who had died in mine cave-ins or from breathing poisonous dust, a by-product of the mining operations. Meanwhile, the Americans who owned the mine grew extremely rich.

The Chuquicamata site was the largest open-pit mine in the world at the time. It produced 20 percent of the world's copper. Members of the Chilean Communist Party wanted to nationalize the mine. In this process, the Chilean government would purchase the operation and run it for the benefit of the nation's citizens rather than for the profit of private owners. The earnings from the mine could be used to build schools and hospitals and to provide social services for average Chilean citizens. Business and government leaders in the United States strongly opposed nationalization. Powerful U.S. politicians had pressured Chile's rulers to outlaw the Communist Party and to arrest those who supported nationalization.

In the 1950s, miners in Central and South America did backbreaking labor by hand. The work was dangerous, and the pay was barely enough to live on.

After speaking to the couple, Guevara began to develop his political awareness. He felt it was wrong for a U.S. company to reap huge profits from Chilean copper.

A **UNITED** LATIN AMERICA

As he witnessed poverty and despair in a land rich with natural resources, Guevara's political opinions continued to develop. He concluded that South America's problems could be solved if all South American people belonged to one common nation. On his twenty-fourth birthday in 1952, Guevara wrote in his diary, "The divisions of [South] America into unstable, [separated] nations is completely fictional. We constitute a single mestizo [mixed European and Indian] race, which from Mexico to the Magellan Straits [southern tip of South America] bears notable [ethnic] similarities. . . . I propose a toast to . . . a United Latin America." Guevara dreamed of a revolution to create a united Latin America (all the nations south of the United States, including Mexico) with no national borders and free of foreign domination.

THE BANANA REPUBLICS

After returning home to Argentina, Guevara continued his studies. He received his doctor's diploma in June 1953. Rather than practicing medicine, he went on a second long voyage outside Argentina. Despite occasional bouts of severe asthma, he traveled to Bolivia, Peru, Ecuador, and the Central America nations of Panama, Guatemala, Nicaragua, and Honduras.

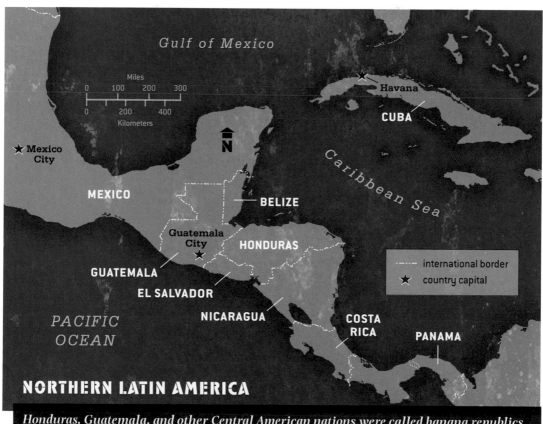

NORTHERN LATIN AMERICA

Honduras, Guatemala, and other Central American nations were called banana republics because their governments were controlled by giant international fruit companies.

Workers harvest bananas at a United Fruit Company plantation in Guatemala in 1945.

Guevara noted that the economic situation in Central America was worse than that of South America. At the time, almost all Central American countries were run by brutal dictators backed by wealthy families and international corporations. The powerful families and corporations ran fruit, vegetable, coffee, and timber businesses. They gave the dictators money and weapons, which enabled them to stay in power. Powerful politicians in the U.S. government also supported this system.

In Nicaragua the Somoza family worked with the U.S. military and the U.S. Central Intelligence Agency (CIA, an agency that gathers information on foreign governments, crime organizations, terrorist organizations, and other potential threats to the United States) to maintain power.

In El Salvador, a single family owned almost all the nation's vast coffee plantations. In Honduras the U.S.-owned United Fruit Company controlled the government and ran the nation's shipping and railroad systems. United Fruit also grew bananas on huge plantations. Because of the influence of United Fruit, Honduras and other Central American nations were often called banana republics.

GUATEMALA'S **STRUGGLE**

When Guevara first visited Guatemala in 1953, the country was struggling to escape its banana republic past. Over the decades, dictators had given the nation's best farmland to United Fruit. As a result, United Fruit owned more land than any other person or group in Guatemala. The company also owned Guatemala's railway, electricity system, and only port.

The situation in Guatemala began to change in 1950, when the nation held free and fair elections. Jacobo Arbenz Guzmán, a former military

THE COLD WAR

In the early 1950s, the Communist Soviet Union (a former nation consisting of modern-day Russia and fourteen other republics) and the capitalist United States stockpiled thousands of nuclear missiles, ready to launch at each other at a moment's notice. But rather than fight a "hot war" with weapons, Soviets and Americans waged a "cold war." During the Cold War (1945–1991), both sides tried to influence business and political policies in Central and South America, as well as in other places around the globe.

In the United States, distrust and hatred of the Soviet Union was widespread. Many Americans believed the Soviets were planning to conquer the world, nation by nation, and to enslave people under the Soviet form of Communism. Americans feared that Communists would take control of all private property, such as houses, farms, newspapers, and factories. Americans also hated the Soviets because their government had banned religious practices and had closed churches, mosques, and temples. The biggest fear for many Americans was that the Soviets would build military bases in Latin American countries. As a result of the Cold War, the CIA and other U.S. organizations insisted on keeping pro-U.S. politicians in power in Latin America, regardless of the brutality or corruption of their rule.

officer, was elected president by an overwhelming majority of voters. Arbenz considered himself a Socialist. Socialists believe that businesses should operate according to principals of fairness for all rather than profits for a few. In a Socialist society, state- and privately owned businesses work together. Socialist countries often raise money through high taxes on individuals and private businesses. The tax money pays for education, health care, and social services.

CAPITALIST OCTOPUSES

Guevara arrived in Guatemala during a very tense period in its history. The year before, in 1952, Arbenz had put in place a series of reforms, giving free farmland to thousands of poor families. To make this possible, the government forced United Fruit and other companies to sell acreage that was not being farmed. Arbenz himself gave up a large plot of family-owned land. Over eighteen months, the land program distributed millions of acres to about one hundred thousand families.

In 1953 United Fruit and U.S. politicians who supported the company began a political and media campaign against Arbenz. Opponents falsely labeled him a Communist. They said Arbenz was allowing the Communist Soviet Union to gain power in Guatemala and to use it as a base to start revolutions in the region. In this era, the United States and the Soviet Union were bitter enemies. The United States was extremely fearful of Communism spreading around the world. In this climate of fear and paranoia, the CIA secretly worked with United Fruit to overthrow the democratically elected Arbenz. The company smuggled weapons into Guatemala on its ships, and the CIA began training military forces in neighboring Nicaragua.

At the same time, thousands of Latin American political activists flooded into Guatemala to observe Arbenz's reforms firsthand. Che Guevara was among them. In a letter to his aunt in Argentina, Guevara explained his reasons for the trip:

> I had the opportunity to pass through the dominions [landholdings] of United Fruit, convincing me once again of just how terrible these capitalist octopuses are. I have sworn . . . that I won't rest until I see these capitalist octopuses annihilated [killed]. In Guatemala I will perfect myself and achieve what I need to be an authentic revolutionary.

EL CHE ARGENTINO

Guevara lived for months in the capital, Guatemala City, developing what he called his "shining faith in the socialist future." During this time, Guevara met with high-level government officials to learn about Guatemala's land reforms.

Guevara also met a group of Cubans who had participated in a failed armed rebellion against the Cuban president, dictator Fulgencio Batista. To avoid arrest and possible execution for their roles in the revolution, the Cubans had become exiles.

Batista was a particularly cruel leader. His police officers tortured prisoners, especially his political enemies. Historians estimate that his regime killed about twenty thousand political prisoners. As in the rest of Latin America, the gap between rich and poor in Cuba was enormous. In the cities, one out of three workers was unemployed. In the countryside, hunger and disease were everywhere. Havana, Cuba's capital, was a seamy, corrupt city, virtually ruled by the U.S. Mafia (a network of organized crime families). Organized crime ran a booming drug trade and made millions of dollars from casinos and prostitution.

Cuban leader Fulgencio Batista, shown here in March 1957, was a brutal dictator.

The failed Cuban rebellion had been led by a former lawyer named Fidel Castro, who then was serving a fifteen-year prison sentence for his revolutionary activities. He and the other Cuban revolutionaries were celebrities among the political activists in Guatemala.

Guevara befriended one of the Cubans, Antonio "Ñico" López. The men had long political discussions late into the night. It was López who gave Guevara his famous nickname, calling him El Che Argentino. *Che* roughly translates to "pal" or "man."

Around this time, friends introduced Guevara to Hilda Gadea, a Peruvian economist working for the Arbenz government. Gadea, an intellectual woman of mixed Chinese and Indian ancestry, was not impressed with Guevara at first. She later wrote, "He seemed too superficial to be an intelligent man, egotistical and conceited." Despite her misgivings, Gadea was soon captivated by the dashing young man. She offered him care and sympathy when he suffered through his many bouts of crippling asthma. But even as their romance grew, Guevara was secretly having a casual affair with another woman, a nurse named Julia Mejía.

In early 1954, the CIA had hundreds of spies in Guatemala City.

> ## "In Guatemala I will perfect myself and achieve what I need to be an authentic revolutionary."
> —Che Guevara

One of those spies was assigned to watch Che Guevara. The CIA agent typed a short profile with basic information about Guevara. He noted that Guevara was a charming twenty-five-year-old Argentinean physician who often met with Cuban revolutionaries and was an outspoken supporter of Socialist president Arbenz.

By this time, Guevara was convinced that the Guatemalan reforms were only the first shot in a long global struggle against oppression. He believed a Cuban revolution would one day succeed and that a world war would someday explode between capitalist and Communist nations. In letters to his parents, Guevara declared himself a Communist and a supporter of the Soviet Union.

FLEEING TO **MEXICO**

On June 16, 1954, two days after Guevara's twenty-sixth birthday, U.S.-backed forces began bombing raids on Guatemala. Guevara was close to the action and wrote excitedly about hearing machine gun fire and bombs exploding. But the violence caused suffering, and the thrill quickly wore off for Che. He put his medical skills to work, helping the wounded.

On June 27, fearful that the U.S. military would soon invade Guatemala, Arbenz resigned rather than risk widespread bloodshed. He fled to Mexico City, Mexico, with his family. Guatemala's new president, Carlos Castillo

A soldier surveys damage to a military fort in Guatemala in July 1954. Guevara witnessed much destruction and violence while living in Guatemala during the U.S.-backed bombing raids.

Armas—handpicked by the CIA—entered the capital a few days later. Castillo Armas announced that he would round up and arrest everyone who supported Arbenz.

Che took refuge in the Argentine embassy and eventually escaped to Mexico City. There, he bought a camera and began working as a freelance photographer. While befriending other Communists and revolutionary thinkers in Mexico's capital city, he spent his days taking pictures at birthday parties and weddings.

CHAPTER TWO

A GUERRILLA WARRIOR

In a revolution, if it's a true
revolution, you win or you die.

—Che Guevara, 1965

By the summer of 1955, Guevara had reunited in Mexico City with some of
his friends from Guatemala. They included Cuban revolutionary Ñico López
and Guevara's girlfriend Hilda Gadea.

During this time, a new face appeared among Guevara's group of
revolutionary exiles. Raúl Castro had also fled Cuba with his brother Fidel.
Guevara and Gadea quickly became friends with Raúl and invited him for
dinner. Gadea noted that the beardless, fair-haired Raúl looked like an
innocent university student, much younger than his twenty-four years. But
he had helped his brother plot the failed rebellion, and according to Gadea,
Raúl had strong political passions:

> [His] ideas were very clear as to how the revolution was to be
> made. . . . He was convinced that in Cuba, as in most of Latin
> America, one could not expect to take power through elections:
> armed struggle was necessary. But this effort must be carried
> out in close union with the populous [people]; power would come
> only with the support of the people. With this, one could go on to
> transform the capitalist society into a new, socialist society.

OPPOSITE: *Fidel Castro's rebel army marches into Havana, Cuba, in 1959.*

THE **JULY 26** MOVEMENT

In June 1955, the Cuban government freed Castro under the condition that he leave the country. Fidel arrived in Mexico City in early July and continued his plans for revolution in Cuba. He named the struggle the July 26 Movement, after the date of the earlier failed rebellion he had led in Cuba. In Mexico City, Castro soon met Guevara. In a 1971 speech, he explained why Guevara was eager to join with the Cuban rebels in their cause:

> *[Because] of the extremely bitter experiences he lived through [in Guatemala]—that cowardly aggression against the country, the interruption of a process that had awakened the hopes of the people—because of his revolutionary vocation [calling], his spirit of struggle, we can't say it took hours, we can say that in a matter of minutes Che decided to join the small group of Cubans who were . . . organizing a new phase of the struggle in our country.*

Guevara and Castro were young. Neither was yet thirty. Both men felt passionately about the cause of revolution. Both men were highly intelligent and driven by fierce egos. Castro told Guevara he wanted to launch a revolution from Mexico. He planned to load a group of armed revolutionaries in a boat and land them on Cuban shores.

At first Guevara wasn't sure he should participate. By this time, he and Gadea were married and expecting a baby. Their daughter, Hilda Beatriz Guevara, was born on February 15, 1956. Although the birth of his daughter brought him great joy, Guevara felt extremely confined by his marriage commitment. Eager to escape the restrictions of family life, he decided to join the revolution. As he wrote his friend Tita Infante,

> *My incapacity to live with the baby's mother is greater than my affection for [the baby]. For a moment I thought that a combination of the little girl's charm and consideration for her mother (who is in many ways a great woman, who loves me in an almost pathological [abnormal] way) might turn me into a boring family man. Now I know this will not be the case.*

A **DISCOURAGING** BEGINNING

In early 1956, dozens of Cuban exiles assembled in Mexico City to train for a violent overthrow of the Batista government in Cuba. A one-eyed Cuban colonel was charged with showing the men techniques of guerrilla, or unconventional, warfare. (The word *guerra* is Spanish for "war"; *guerrilla* means "little war." Guerrilla warfare involves small groups of fighters using ambushes, raids, bombings, and other small-scale tactics.) Castro hired Guevara as the troop doctor, but he was also one of the most dedicated soldiers during training.

Guevara's involvement with Castro did not escape the attention of the CIA. In June an agent added another page to his file. He described Guevara as "an Argentine Communist . . . [connected] with the Fidel Castro plot against President Batista of Cuba."

Castro bought a battered 38-foot (11-meter) yacht, naming it *Granma* after his grandmother. On the night of November 24, 1956, the Cuban Revolution began.

Both Castro (left) and Guevara (right), shown dressing after a night in a jail in Mexico City, were young and idealistic when they launched the Cuban Revolution.

Eighty-one men, including Guevara and the Castro brothers, set sail from the city of Tuxpan on the Gulf of Mexico coast. Dozens of men on the leaky, overcrowded boat became seasick on the churning ocean. While the other revolutionaries clutched their stomachs in anguish, Guevara struggled with asthma. He realized, too late, that he had forgotten his asthma medicine.

On the rough seas, the planned five-day journey took seven days. Without his medicine, Guevara spent much of this time coughing, wheezing, and gasping for air. When the revolutionaries finally reached Cuba's west coast, they landed in a mosquito-filled swamp, made nearly impassible by the tangled roots of mangrove trees. U.S. intelligence forces had learned of the invasion and notified Batista. His forces circled the skies in helicopters. Although the guerrillas were able to elude the Cuban soldiers under the cover of dense trees in the swamp, the guerrillas were in rough shape. The hard ocean voyage and slog through the swamp had exhausted them. Their food and water supplies were depleted. But they managed to escape to the isolated Sierra Maestra range at the southern tip of the island.

After two weeks of hard cross-country marching, the revolutionaries found a remote area to set up camp. They were soon joined by new Cuban volunteers, who brought weapons, ammunition, and food. In mid-January 1957, the group attacked a small military outpost, killing several Cuban soldiers. In the following days, Guevara dodged bullets from Cuban soldiers and killed a man in battle for the first time.

A **DEDICATED** FANATIC

The July 26 Movement quickly gained support from Cuban students, poor people, and intellectuals. Many Cubans saw the revolutionaries as romantic outlaws. Batista tried to stop the growing revolutionary movement by making false statements. He announced in newspapers that the military had killed Fidel Castro and destroyed his guerrilla army. Batista's move proved to be embarrassing when Castro confirmed that he was very much alive. In mid-February, *New York Times* reporter Herbert Matthews interviewed the guerrilla leader. Matthews wrote:

> *The personality of the man [Fidel Castro] is overpowering. It was easy to see . . . why he has caught the imagination of the youth of Cuba all over the island. Here was an educated, dedicated fanatic, a man of ideals, of courage, and of remarkable qualities of leadership.*

COMANDANTE GUEVARA

By mid-April, the dashing, cigar-smoking Fidel Castro had become an international star. Fearful of, yet fascinated by, Castro, U.S. TV and radio reporters traveled to Cuba to seek interviews with the revolutionary. The publicity attracted more rebels to the cause.

Young men with idealistic notions of revolution tracked through the forests of southern Cuba to join the July 26 Movement. Many new recruits were from Cuba's two largest cities, Havana and Santiago de Cuba. A few were white college students from the United States, attracted by the revolutionaries' fight for economic justice.

Fidel Castro poses in front of a tank in January 1959.

Guevara's task was interviewing the rookie guerrillas. First, he had to decide if they were spies. Next, he taught the recruits about the political beliefs and motives of the revolutionaries. Many of the guerrillas were illiterate, so Guevara also held classes under the trees, teaching guerrillas to read and write. Guevara's tasks in the July 26 Movement were summed up in his description of one recruit, Roberto Rodríguez, nicknamed Vaquerito, or "Little Cowboy." He wrote, "Vaquerito did not have a political idea in his head, nor did he seem to be anything other than a happy, healthy boy, who saw all of this as a marvelous adventure. He came barefoot and [we] lent him a pair of shoes."

"Here was an educated, dedicated fanatic, a man of ideals, of courage, and of remarkable qualities of leadership."

—Herbert Matthews

In July 1957, Castro's forces attacked a remote Cuban military outpost. Guevara was given the task of rescuing guerrillas wounded in the fight and transporting them back to base camp. He performed well, and Castro promoted him to captain several days after his birthday. He took charge of a column of seventy-five men. Soon Castro promoted Guevara again, to *comandante,* or commander, the highest rank within the rebel army. With this position, Guevara wore a black beret adorned with a red, five-pointed star. The star was a symbol of Communism, with each point representing one finger on a worker's hand. This hat quickly became part of Guevara's iconic image.

GUEVARA'S GUERRILLA WARFARE

In 1960 Che Guevara wrote a short text titled *Guerrilla Warfare: A Method*, in which he recounted lessons learned during the revolutionary battle for Cuba in the late 1950s. In this excerpt, Guevara discusses the importance of peasant support:

[This] great mass earns its livelihood by working as peons [servants] on the plantations for the most miserable wages, or they work the soil under conditions of exploitation indistinguishable from those of the Middle Ages [around 500 to 1500 in Europe].

These are the circumstances which determine that the poor population of the countryside constitutes a tremendous potential revolutionary force. The armies are set up and equipped for conventional warfare. They are the force whereby the power of the exploiting classes is maintained. When they are confronted with the irregular warfare of peasants based on their own home grounds, they become absolutely powerless; they lose ten men for every revolutionary fighter who falls. Demoralization among them mounts rapidly when they are beset by an invisible and invincible army which provides them no chance to display their military-academy tactics and their fanfare of war, of which they boast so much to repress the city workers and students.

The initial struggle of small fighting units is constantly nurtured by new forces; the mass movement begins to grow bold, the old order bit by bit breaks up into a thousand pieces.

During the Cuban Revolution, Guevara often wore a beret with a red, five-pointed star—a symbol of Communism.

IMPOSING AN IRON FIST

As a commander, Guevara had to deal with problems within his own ranks. Many city boys attracted to the romantic guerrilla movement were unable to tolerate tough military discipline and harsh living conditions. A growing number deserted. Some men attracted to the rebel movement were petty criminals, social outcasts, or former convicts—men with little to lose by defying the government. These men thought nothing of robbing, raping, and terrorizing local peasants. Their actions hurt the movement, which was trying to gain the loyalty and respect of the people. *Chivatos,* or spies, were also a problem. Rebel soldiers provided information about guerrilla training and troop positions to Batista's military, often in exchange for money.

Guevara was a tough commander and wrote about the need for strict obedience: "[The situation] called for an iron fist. We were obliged to inflict . . . punishment [as a warning to others] in order to curb all violations of discipline and to eliminate the seeds of anarchy [lawlessness], which sprang up in areas lacking a stable government."

Guevara had little tolerance for deserters, chivatos, or criminals.

He set up a system to try those men. Those found guilty were usually executed with a gunshot to the head. Guevara himself was often the executioner. He quickly earned a reputation as a hard-hearted commander who left a trail of dead deserters and chivatos throughout the Sierra Maestra. For this reason, a February 1958 CIA report on Guevara gave him the title Henchman of Fidel Castro.

By October 1957, Guevara's tough, disciplined troops had established a base camp called El Hombrito. Guevara built the camp as a model city, what he hoped all of Cuba would be like after the revolution. He set up a bakery, a small weapons repair workshop, a leather and shoemaking facility, and a cigar-making production line. He established a school to teach reading, writing, history, and Communist politics. Guevara also wrote a newsletter called the *Free Cuban,* which political activists distributed throughout the region. Many locals who visited El Hombrito were impressed and were eager to join the revolution.

AN ADVENTURING SPIRIT

By 1958 Che Guevara's CIA file was growing daily. The following excerpt, written by an unnamed CIA spy, attempts to explain Guevara's motives for leading the revolution:

"Che" has a conception of himself as a romantic, dashing, warrior figure. He claims that he has no political influence over Castro and that he does not want any. Politics, as such, does not interest him . . . if Castro wins his fight he ("Che") will leave Cuba and explore the upper reaches of the Amazon River. However, "Che" now considers himself a Cuban and as of the present moment intends to become a Cuban citizen after Castro wins his rebellion (which "Che" is sure he will). . . . He is an adventurer, not a politician or a professional revolutionary. "Che" has always been searching for something with which to give his life some meaning and significance and that for the time being he has found it in Castro, not Castro the politician, but in Castro the underdog, in Castro the fighter against tyranny. He is an individualist, "Che" stated more than once. . . . [If] Castro's rebellion does not succeed, he, "Che," will "die like a man" at the head of his troops. . . . If this sounds romantic, "Che" is a romantic.

From their base in the Sierra Maestra, the Cuban revolutionaries moved on to take Santa Clara and finally Havana, the Cuban capital. U.S. leaders worried about the revolution taking place in a country so close to Miami, Florida.

BUILDING A MODEL SOCIETY

In November 1957, almost a year after the July 26 Movement arrived in Cuba, Batista ordered ten thousand soldiers to seek out and destroy Castro's army of about 320 guerrillas. The soldiers invaded and overran El Hombrito. Most of the guerrillas there escaped into the surrounding highlands. Guevara was shot in the foot but was not seriously wounded. He regrouped with his men at another base camp. In May 1958, the Cuban military again made plans to encircle the rebel forces in the mountains and destroy them.

However, in July, columns led by Castro and Guevara attacked Cuban military camps and forced the surrender of hundreds of troops. By August Batista's forces had completely withdrawn from the Sierra Maestra region. In the following weeks, many government soldiers and officers switched sides and joined the revolutionaries. Castro used the new troops to capture ground in areas close to large cities.

Following the methods he pioneered in El Hombrito, Guevara set up a model camp with small industries and a military training center in Cabellete de Cases. There he met twenty-four-year-old Aleida March, described by

In the Sierra Maestra, Guevara and his men lived in wooden huts and used mules to transport their equipment.

Italian journalist Franco Pierini as "one of the most beautiful women in Cuba." March was a teacher from an upper-class background who had quit her job to join the revolution. Although Guevara was still married to Hilda Gadea, he and March quickly became inseparable. March remembered how the two met. One night, the noise and excitement of a guerrilla offensive left her unable to sleep. So she sat by the side of a road as the sun came up. Guevara pulled up in a jeep and said, "I'm going to attack [the city of] Cabaiguán, want to come along? Sure [I replied] and from that moment on I never left his side—or let him out of my sight." Che soon divorced Hilda and married Aleida.

Che Guevara and Aleida March (center front) were married at La Cabaña Fortress in 1959. Raúl Castro and his wife stand to the left of Guevara.

WINNING **THE WAR**

In the days that followed, March was eyewitness to some of the most exciting—and most dangerous—action of the guerrilla war. On December 16, Guevara's fighters blew up roads and rail lines around Santa Clara, a major city in the central part of the island. In the area around Santa Clara, about 350 revolutionaries overran twelve army and police posts. They took eight hundred prisoners, with only eleven guerrillas killed.

The Cuban military reacted by sending an armored train loaded with weapons, ammunition, and communications equipment to defend Santa Clara. On December 29, Guevara targeted the train. He had his rebel soldiers bulldoze the rail lines on the outskirts of the city. When the train derailed as planned, the guerrillas attacked soldiers in the train with Molotov cocktails (bottles of burning gasoline). Guevara described the horrific scene:

> [The] men in the armored train had been dislodged by our Molotov cocktails; in spite of their excellent protection they were prepared to fight only at long range, from comfortable positions, and against a virtually unarmed enemy. . . . Harassed by our men who . . . were hurling bottles of flaming gasoline, the train—thanks to its armor-plate—became a veritable oven for its soldiers.

The victory outside Santa Clara was a major milestone of the revolutionary war. The guerrillas captured a massive array of weaponry from

Crowds gather on the street in 1959 as Castro's victorious revolutionary troops ride captured tanks into the city of Santa Clara.

the train, including bazookas, mortars, machine guns, cannons, and more than one million rounds of ammunition.

Although Havana was still in the hands of government forces, on New Year's Eve, Batista realized that defeat was imminent. He resigned and handed over control of the government to his generals. The next day, January 1, 1959, Batista fled Cuba in an airplane packed with forty family members and friends. When news of Batista's exit reached government garrisons (military forts),

thousands of Cuban soldiers laid down their arms. In Santa Clara, Havana, and other cities, citizens streamed into the streets, cheering in celebration. Castro organized his victorious troops and marched into the capital, followed soon after by Che and Aleida.

In victory, the small guerrilla force was now in charge of a nation of six million people. Guevara understood that the hardest work was yet to come. He told a friend "We've won the war, now we have to start the revolution."

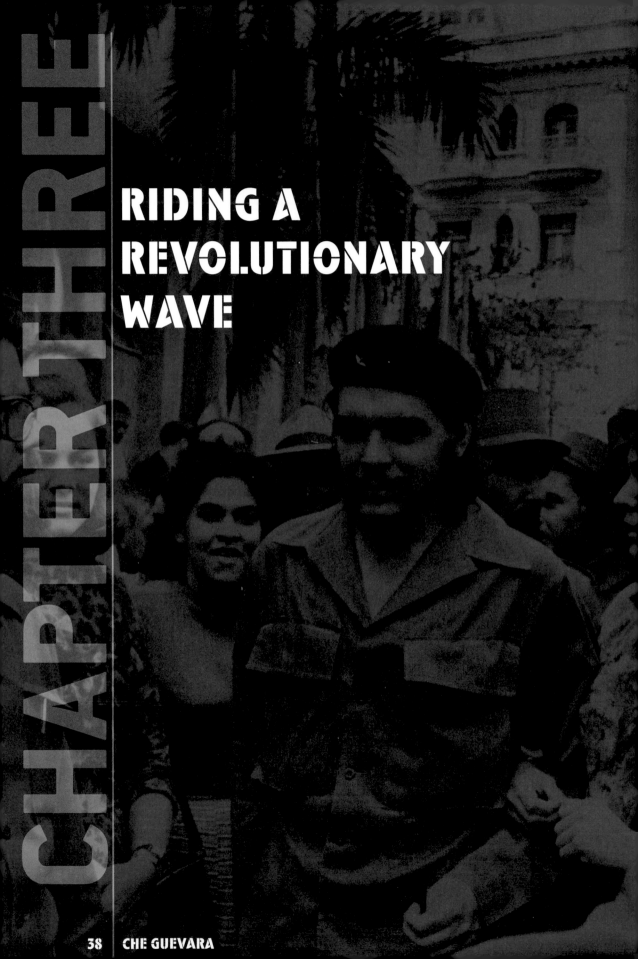

CHAPTER THREE

RIDING A REVOLUTIONARY WAVE

> We were convinced that the destiny of Cuba was to inspire revolution.... Everywhere there was a tyrant, a Latin American dictator, he was automatically our enemy.
>
> —Osvaldo de Cárdenas, Cuban intelligence agent, 1960

When the revolutionary government took power in Cuba in early January 1959, Che Guevara and Fidel Castro became celebrities almost overnight. Delirious crowds danced in the streets of Havana. International reporters poured into the country to interview the bearded, cigar-smoking revolutionaries, who were widely viewed as romantic warriors in pursuit of justice. Guevara, with his sly smile, messy hair, and black beret with its red star of revolution, caught the eye of countless photographers. His photo appeared on the front pages of magazines and newspapers throughout the world.

Millions of struggling peasants, from Latin America to Asia and the Middle East, instantly identified with the revolutionaries in Cuba. Guevara's words, written three weeks after the rebel victory, raised hopes around the globe:

We have demonstrated that a small group of men who are determined, supported by the people, and without fear of dying . . . can overcome a regular army. . . . There is another [lesson] for our brothers . . . which is we must make agrarian [farm-based] revolutions, fight in the fields, in the mountains, and from here take the revolution to the cities.

OPPOSITE: *Guevara walks through a jubilant crowd of people in Havana after the revolutionaries take the city in early 1959.*

Guevara was an iron-fisted commander. He oversaw the killing of former Batista officials, soldiers, and police officers.

THE SUPREME **PROSECUTOR**

Castro made himself prime minister of Cuba and commander in chief of the new Cuban military, called the Revolutionary Armed Forces. Recognizing Guevara's strict adherence to military discipline during the uprising, Castro made him chief of the Department of Training of the Revolutionary Armed Forces. In this role, Guevara's duties included training and educating soldiers. Guevara also became commander of La Cabaña Fortress, the largest military prison in Cuba.

La Cabaña Fortress held more than one thousand prisoners of war, most of them former Batista officials. The prisoners included corrupt government bureaucrats, chivatos, military personnel, and torturers who had worked for Batista's police department. Castro decided to conduct trials for these people, whom he considered traitors and war criminals. Guevara took charge of a military tribunal (court) known as the Cleansing Commission. As the chief judge of the Cleansing Commission, he oversaw trials and decided the guilt or innocence of each prisoner.

Every trial before the Cleansing Commission lasted about four hours. The commission sentenced more than fifty prisoners to death by firing squad. Several hundred more were tried and executed elsewhere in Cuba. Guevara never wrote about his experiences as leader of the tribunal, and historical accounts are mixed. Some exiled Batista supporters said that Guevara delighted in interrogating prisoners, organizing trials, and issuing execution orders. Orlando Borrego, a member of the Cleansing Commission, has a different opinion. Borrego says Che made every effort to maintain neutrality so that innocent people would not be put to death. According to Borrego:

> [Our] paramount [main] concerns were [to ensure] that the sense of revolutionary morality and of justice prevailed, that no injustice was committed. In that, Che was very careful. . . . [If a prisoner was accused of] extreme torture and killings and deaths, then yes— they were condemned to death. . . . [All] the relatives of the dead, or tortured person came, or the tortured person himself, and in the tribunal, displaying his body, he would reveal the tortures that he had received.

A large majority of Cubans supported the work of the Cleansing Commission. They believed the executions were fair and just, given the crimes they felt the prisoners had committed during Batista's regime. Crowds gathered outside the fortress each night and cheered as fusillades (shots) from the firing squad rang out.

"[Our] paramount [main] concerns were [to ensure] that the sense of revolutionary morality and of justice prevailed, that no injustice was committed. In that, Che was very careful."

—Orlando Borrego

DID YOU SAY "ECONOMIST"?

Several years after the Cuban Revolution, a reporter asked Guevara why a person who was trained as a doctor was put in charge of Cuba's complex economy. Guevara displayed his well-known sense of humor in answering the question. He said that in 1960, Castro held a meeting to appoint someone president of the national bank. Castro asked, "Is there an economist in the room?" Guevara raised his hand. Castro immediately made him bank president. After the meeting, Castro said, "Che, I didn't know you were an economist." "Economist?" Che replied. "I thought you said *communist*."

REVOLUTIONARY
SCHEMING

In 1959 Castro made Che Guevara an honorary Cuban citizen. Castro also put Guevara in charge of the Cuban economy. Around this time, Guevara wrote a short book called *Guerrilla Warfare: A Method* based on notes taken during the armed resistance. The twenty-seven-page manual describes in detail the successful tactics Guevara developed to fight the Cuban army. It contains instructions for making bombs, planting land mines, committing sabotage (destroying the enemy's property to cripple its war effort), and using terrorism against government forces.

Guerrilla Warfare alarmed observers in the United States. They feared Guevara was using his position to incite revolution throughout Latin America. In early 1960, Daniel Braddock, a U.S. State Department official, described Guevara's intentions in a memo to the CIA and top U.S. military officials. Braddock noted that Guevara had summoned Latin American revolutionaries to Havana from the Dominican Republic, Nicaragua, Paraguay, and Haiti. During their visit, Guevara personally organized, trained, and provided financial assistance to the guerrillas. He was particularly interested in launching a guerrilla invasion of Nicaragua. If successful, the invasion would allow him to use the country as a base for revolution throughout the Northern Hemisphere. Braddock concluded the memo with the warning:

"Cuba will be a center for revolutionary scheming and activities for some time, with consequent concern and difficulties for various governments, including our own."

Guevara's revolutionary intentions were being studied by those in the highest levels of the U.S. government. Another memo from the U.S. Embassy in Havana noted that Guevara, with his control over the Cuban armed forces, represented the single most important danger in the spread of Communism in Latin America. As Guevara biographer Jon Lee Anderson writes, "Perhaps more than Fidel himself, Che was well on his way to becoming Washington's number one nemesis [enemy] in Latin America."

Guevara traveled to other Communist countries, including China. Here he meets with Chinese finance minister Li Hsein-nien (left) in 1960.

THWARTING THE CIA

Castro and Guevara made many powerful enemies in a very short period. They oversaw agricultural reform in Cuba, seizing private land from wealthy farmers and giving it to poor peasants. They took control of private industries—including U.S.-owned oil refineries, sugar plantations, and mines. They also closed down the Mafia-controlled gambling industry and luxury hotels.

Castro's rule became increasingly repressive. He imprisoned or executed anyone who opposed his policies. As a result, thousands of anti-Communist Cubans fled their homeland for nearby Miami, Florida. Meanwhile, the CIA closely monitored Guevara, who made frequent trips to the Soviet Union, where he purchased tanks, airplanes, missiles, and other armaments.

Within Cuba, Castro and Guevara's enemies got organized. In February 1961, five anti-Communist Cuban gunmen hid behind some bushes near Guevara's home, planning to assassinate him. The men were apparently unaware that Guevara had already left home for work. At home was Aleida, who had recently had a baby. One of Guevara's

neighbors, an army officer, saw the men and opened fire with an automatic weapon. A wild gunfight erupted. Inside the Guevara home, Aleida grabbed the baby and, with nanny Sofía Gato, crawled under a stairwell to hide. The army officer and two of the gunmen were killed. Three other gunmen escaped.

Far from Havana, CIA agents and Mafia bosses in Chicago, Illinois, were also making plans to eliminate the Cuban revolutionary leaders. They came up with plots that included slipping Castro an exploding cigar and dropping poison pills into his drink.

But Castro had a vast and effective spy network, which discovered the amateurish Mafia and CIA assassination attempts. Castro's security team thwarted all of them. However, other U.S. agents put together a much more serious plan to overthrow the revolutionary government of Cuba. The CIA recruited fifteen hundred Cuban exiles, called Brigade 2506, and armed and trained them in Panama, Guatemala, and Florida. Brigade 2506 invaded Cuba on April 17, 1961, landing at the Bay of Pigs, a beach south of Havana, just after midnight.

The Bay of Pigs invasion was a disaster. The Soviet intelligence agency, the KGB, learned of the

ASSASSINATION ATTEMPTS

In the early 1960s, Robert F. Kennedy, the U.S. president's brother, was the U.S. attorney general. According to official documents released in the 1970s, Kennedy authorized the CIA to work with various members of the Mafia to assassinate Fidel Castro. The plots ranged from dangerous to ridiculous.

In one attempt, two powerful Mafia bosses working with the CIA gave one of Castro's ex-girlfriends poison pills to drop into his drink. She smuggled the pills into Castro's bedroom in a jar of cold cream, but they melted in the jar.

Other plots never got beyond the planning stage. The CIA considered slipping the dictator the powerful hallucinogenic drug LSD before an important speech, so he would appear deranged. It also wanted to dust Castro's trademark bushy beard with a poisonous substance to make it fall out, embarrassing him. While these plots never came to pass, the CIA, the Mafia, and other hit men, spies, and angry Cuban citizens made hundreds of attempts to kill the Cuban president.

plan well in advance and warned the Cuban government. When Brigade 2506 landed, Cuban forces repelled the attackers, killing more than one hundred and taking twelve hundred prisoners.

THE **MISSILE** CRISIS

Although unsuccessful, the Bay of Pigs operation showed that Cuba had much to fear from the United States. Needing a strong ally, the Cubans established even closer relations with the Soviet Union. Guevara's trips to the Soviet capital city Moscow, Russia, became more frequent. By the summer of 1962, the Soviets were supplying Cuba with many basic necessities, including oil, wheat, machinery, and millions of dollars in loans. In addition, the Soviets were buying all the Cuban sugar formerly sold to the United States.

While Guevara made deals to bolster the Cuban economy, he also made a more menacing bargain. As many Americans feared, Guevara invited the Soviets to build military bases in Cuba. In September 1962, Soviet warships began delivering nuclear missiles and mobile missile launchers

A group of Castro's soldiers pose for a photograph in April 1961, after routing the U.S.-backed invasion at the Bay of Pigs.

to Cuba. These dangerous weapons could have completely destroyed Washington, D.C., or New York City in a matter of minutes.

On October 14, the United States learned of the missiles, setting off an incident called the Cuban Missile Crisis. U.S. president John F. Kennedy ordered the U.S. Navy to blockade Cuba—preventing Soviet navy ships from leaving or entering Havana ports. News of the blockade alarmed people around the world. They feared the Soviet and U.S. battleships would start

firing at each other, setting off a conflict that could lead to nuclear war.

In the tense days that followed, millions of people were glued to their radios and televisions waiting for the latest news. Castro believed the United States was about to drop nuclear bombs on Cuba. He urged Soviet premier Nikita Khrushchev to launch a first strike. Khrushchev rejected the idea and made a secret deal with Kennedy without informing Castro or Guevara. The Soviets would withdraw the missiles from Cuba in exchange for a U.S. commitment not to invade Cuba again. In addition, the United States would remove some of its nuclear missiles from Turkey, which bordered the Soviet Union. The crisis was averted.

A **CAGED** LION

The Cuban Missile Crisis was resolved peacefully, but Guevara felt that Cuba had been used as a pawn in a game between the superpowers. As Castro moved closer to the Soviets, Guevara began losing interest in Cuban politics.

Peace activists in the United States implore President Kennedy not to let the Cuban Missile Crisis erupt into nuclear war.

He was tired of working eighteen-hour days in an office and longed to once again lead a guerrilla army on mountain maneuvers. In 1964 Uruguayan writer Eduardo Galeano described Guevara's unhappiness: "Che was not a desk man: he was a creator of revolutions. . . . Somehow, that tension of a caged lion . . . had to explode. He needed the sierra [mountains]."

RAISING THE ANTE AT THE UNITED NATIONS

Tired of his desk job, Guevara traveled the world, visiting Algeria, Switzerland, and other nations. He delivered angry speeches that criticized both Soviet Communism and U.S. capitalism. Guevara voiced strong support for revolutionary guerrillas fighting in Nicaragua; Guatemala; Venezuela; and in the African nations of Congo, Angola, and Mozambique.

On December 11, 1964, Guevara made a historic trip to the New York City headquarters of the United Nations. He combed his hair, trimmed his beard, polished his boots, and pressed his military fatigues for his appearance before the international peacekeeping organization. He addressed world leaders in an hour-long speech. In it, he criticized the growing number of CIA advisers in the Southeast Asian nation of Vietnam, which was then caught in a vicious war (1957–1975) between Communist and non-Communist forces. He denounced U.S. interference in Latin America. Guevara described nearly every struggle against foreign domination in the world, including conflicts in the Middle East, the Caribbean, the Americas, Asia, and Africa. He concluded the speech with the prediction that revolutionary armies would one day destroy capitalism.

> "Che was not a desk man: he was a creator of revolutions."
>
> —Eduardo Galeano

Even as he spoke at the United Nations, enemies made more attempts on Guevara's life. In one, a twenty-four-year-old Cuban exile, Molly Gonzales, attempted to enter the UN building with a hunting knife. After a short scuffle with police, Gonzales was arrested. She told a reporter who witnessed the incident that she had intended to stab Guevara. In a more serious attempt, an unknown assailant launched a single shell from a bazooka across the East River toward the United Nations. The shell fell short of its target, exploding harmlessly in the river and sending up a geyser of water. The blast rattled the UN windows at the same time Guevara was denouncing the United States in his speech. When he was later told about

Dressed in crisp military fatigues, Guevara speaks at the United Nations on December 11, 1964.

the two assassination attempts, Guevara stated, "It is better to be killed by a woman with a knife than by a man with a gun."

DISAPPEARING **ACT**

After Guevara's UN appearance, he left for a three-month lecture tour in Africa, China, France, Czechoslovakia, and Ireland. While visiting countries on the African continent, Guevara told audiences that Cuba's liberation struggle was similar to those taking place in Africa. He promised that Cuba would assist struggling fighters with training, money, and arms.

When Guevara returned to Cuba on March 15, the press was filming as he deplaned. The homecoming was the last time the public would see Guevara alive. Two weeks later, Guevara left his office at Cuba's Industry Ministry,

THE HOUR HAS COME

At the end of his long speech before the United Nations on December 11, 1964, Che Guevara renamed Latin America the Free Territory of America. He proclaimed freedom for its masses with these words:

[From] one end of the continent to the other [the people] are signaling with clarity that the hour has come—the hour of their vindication [freedom]. . . . Anxious hands are stretched forth, ready to die for what is theirs, to win those rights that were laughed at by one and all for 500 years [since Europeans arrived in the Americas]. Yes, now history will have to take the poor of America into account, the exploited and spurned of America, who have decided to begin writing their history for themselves for all time. . . . [Already] they can be seen carrying signs, slogans, flags; letting them flap in the mountain or prairie winds. And the wave of anger, of demands for justice, of claims for rights trampled underfoot, which is beginning to sweep the lands of Latin America, will not stop. That wave will swell with every passing day. . . . For this great mass of humanity has said, "Enough!" and has begun to march. . . . They will die for their own true and never-to-be-surrendered independence.

claiming he was off to check on rural sugar production. In the following days, the revolutionary leader made top-secret plans to disappear. Guevara told Aleida he was leaving the country. She begged him not to go.

On March 31, Guevara's last day in Cuba, he had lunch with Aleida. Sofía Gato later reported that while she was serving the meal, Guevara asked her what had happened to women whose husbands had died fighting in the Cuban Revolution. Gato replied that most had remarried. Guevara pointed to his coffee cup and said, "In that case, this coffee you serve me, may you serve it to another." The blood drained from Aleida's face. With this comment, Guevara gave her his blessing to marry another if he died. By then the couple had four children. The next day, April 1, he left his home forever.

In the months that followed Guevara's disappearance, his fate was the subject of high drama and swirling worldwide rumors. When asked, even Aleida said she did not know what had happened to him. In October 1965, as questions intensified, Castro read an undated letter, said to be from Guevara, on Cuban TV. In it, Guevara declared his work in Cuba was done. He said he intended to devote himself to bringing about a worldwide revolution. Guevara also announced his resignation from the Cuban government and military and gave up his Cuban citizenship. After years as the world's most visible face of revolution, Che Guevara had vanished, seemingly into thin air.

CHAPTER FOUR

DAYS OF ANGUISH

It must be said with all sincerity that in a true revolution, to which one gives oneself completely...the task of the vanguard [groundbreaking] revolutionary is both magnificent and anguishing.

—Che Guevara, March 12, 1965

By 1965 Che Guevara was one of the most famous living revolutionaries in the world. To some, his actions in Cuba were heroic beyond measure. Guevara's words mesmerized millions of college students, who hoped that they too might become dashing radicals.

Guevara's high profile on the world stage made his sudden disappearance from the public in March 1965 all the more dramatic. He had powerful enemies within the CIA. The U.S. Mafia and thousands of anti-Communists in Cuba and the United States wanted Guevara dead. His political agitation had even angered leaders in the Soviet Union.

Rumors flew. Had Guevara been killed in Cuba on Soviet orders? Or had he died in a revolt in the Dominican Republic? Was he a prisoner in Peru? Hiding out in Argentina? Fighting with Vietnamese Communists?

While the CIA and the KGB were trying to track down Guevara, he shaved his beard, cut his hair, and put on the clothes of an ordinary businessman. He called himself Ramón Benítez and headed to the African nation of Congo. There, Guevara and about one hundred Cuban soldiers worked for more than seven months training a band of Congolese revolutionaries to overthrow Congo's corrupt government. But the effort was doomed. Guevara found that the Congolese guerrillas were often drunk, disorganized, and dishonest

OPPOSITE: *Che Guevara relaxes on a fishing trip in the waters off Cojimar, Cuba, in 1963.*

Guevara (left) poses with a soldier and a baby in Congo, where he tried to organize a revolution in 1965 and 1966. The effort was unsuccessful.

that they lacked revolutionary passion. While training the guerrillas, Guevara came down with a devastating case of dysentery, a sometimes deadly intestinal disease. His weight fell from about 150 pounds (68 kilograms) to only about 110 pounds (50 kg).

Sometime around the middle of 1966, while fighting his illness, Guevara decided to leave Africa—secretly. He headed for Cuba, where he took on yet another false identity. He donned eyeglasses, shaved the top of his head, and put gray streaks in his remaining hair. Using a counterfeit passport, he flew to La Paz, Bolivia, on November 3, 1966.

ANOTHER VIETNAM

Guevara planned to assemble a team of guerrillas in Bolivia to ignite the pan-Latin American revolution that had fired his dreams for so long. The Bolivian government, run by a repressive military general, had strong ties to the United States. By creating unrest in Bolivia, Guevara was sure he could lure the United States into an expensive, drawn-out war, similar to the one it was fighting in Vietnam. Guevara believed a war in Bolivia would damage the United States economically while destroying U.S. influence in Latin America.

Guevara had grand plans, money provided by Castro, and political support from allies in the United States and Europe. By January 1, 1967, he had set up his guerrilla base camp in a desolate, mountain region called Ñancahuazú. Guevara assembled a small army—sixteen Cubans, three Peruvians, and twenty-nine Bolivians—who called themselves the National Liberation Army (ELN, or Ejercito de Liberacion Nacional in Spanish). At first, Guevara went by his alias Ramón. Only the Cuban guerrillas knew his true identity.

From the start, Guevara's band of guerrillas was short on key supplies, such as guns, bullets, radios, clothing, boots, and tents. In addition, Guevara made a major tactical error when he chose Ñancahuazú as a base of operations. The terrain was even more rugged than the Sierra Maestra in Cuba.

Ñancahuazú lies between the towering Andes Mountains and the dense rain forest surrounding the Amazon River. In this area, the guerrillas faced steep ravines, raging rivers, heat, dust, monstrous flies, biting mosquitoes, and stinging beetles. To travel undercover, the guerrillas had to slash through walls of vines and skin-piercing, razor-sharp thorns. When Mario Monje, head of Bolivia's Communist Party, visited the ELN base camp, he told Guevara, "You've fallen into a trap here."

"COLD-BLOODED KILLING MACHINE"

While Che Guevara was seen as a romantic, selfless revolutionary, critics point out that he glorified hatred and violence. In an April 1965 article, Guevara himself wrote:

Hatred [is] an element of struggle; unbending hatred for the enemy, which pushes a human being beyond his natural limitations, making him into an effective, violent, selective, and cold-blooded killing machine. This is what our soldiers must become.

SENDING IN THE TROOPS

During the Cuban Revolution of the late 1950s, Guevara had had support from both rural peasants and people in major cities. Supporters had supplied the guerrillas with food, money, and information about the enemy. In Bolivia, Guevara found—to his surprise—that he could not muster much support from anyone. Local farmers in Ñancahuazú had no idea why the heavily armed guerrillas were in their desolate villages. The peasants did not assume that Guevara and his men were there to free them from grinding poverty and exploitation. Instead, they thought Guevara's fighters were an organized band of cocaine traffickers. The peasants turned the ELN rebels in to the Bolivian military. On March 23, 1967, sixty government soldiers marched into the hills where the ELN was hiding to arrest the guerrillas.

Using fighting tactics perfected in Cuba, Guevara's men hid behind rocks and ambushed the government soldiers. They killed seven and captured the others. Guevara questioned the prisoners. He learned that the Bolivian government, the CIA, and U.S. military advisers knew of his presence in Bolivia and had plans to encircle the guerrillas and wipe them out.

Guevara (seated at right) believed that local farmers would join a revolution in Bolivia. But most Bolivians were suspicious of Guevara and his fighters.

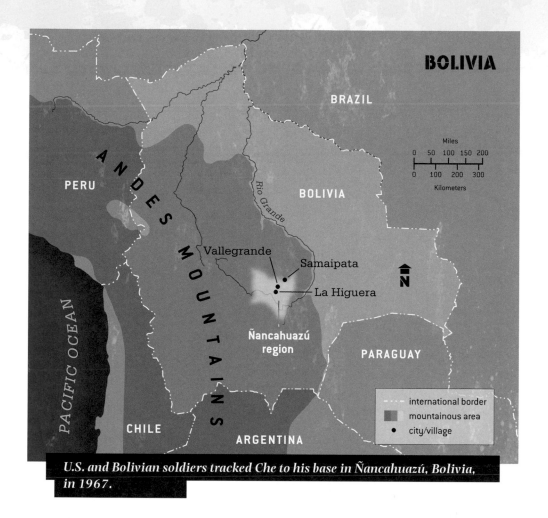

U.S. and Bolivian soldiers tracked Che to his base in Ñancahuazú, Bolivia, in 1967.

HIRING A SPY

In mid-1967, a detachment of elite U.S. Army Rangers called the Green Berets arrived in Bolivia. Their mission was to train and work with Bolivian soldiers to defeat Che and his guerrilla fighters. The Rangers recruited several Cuban agents to accompany them. One was a Cuban exile named Felix Rodríguez, who had a long history of working with the CIA.

In the mid-1960s, Rodríguez had performed covert (undercover), anti-Castro missions for Operation 40, a top-secret unit of the CIA. He worked from secret CIA bases in Nicaragua, Costa Rica, and Miami, where he trained counterrevolutionary commando units. They learned techniques of sabotage, terrorism, guerrilla combat, and other unconventional warfare. Rodríguez also became an expert at gathering intelligence about the enemy through the interrogation of prisoners, electronic eavesdropping, and intercepting mail and other written communications.

In 1967 Rodríguez put his intelligence expertise to use when he traveled to Bolivia as a CIA agent. He assumed a false name and posed sometimes as a Cuban American businessman and sometimes as a Bolivian army officer. He trained an elite group of ten Bolivian soldiers, who worked in guerrilla territory dressed as civilians (nonsoldiers). Their job was to gather intelligence (information) on Guevara and his small band of fighters. Rodríguez explained the value of such intelligence:

> [The] papers in a guerrilla's knapsack are often more valuable than gold. They provide valuable intelligence as to how and where he operated, who his colleagues and collaborators are, and what he is thinking. They also give you detailed clues to his personality and to the strategy he plans to use against you. His wallet often contains pictures and notes that allow you to learn about his personal life— elements you can put into play during interrogation. . . . By reacting swiftly to newly captured information, you may be able to launch a successful operation against a guerrilla unit that only hours before seemingly could not be located.

WHITE BREAD TALKS

The earliest intelligence about Guevara came from the arrest of Régis Debray, a French Communist. Debray was a strong supporter of the Cuban Revolution. In 1966 he had traveled to Bolivia, posing as a French journalist investigating the lives of impoverished tin miners there. In reality, he was hiring soldiers for Guevara and scouting the hills for bases of operation. In addition, the Frenchman acted as a courier, transporting money from Cuba to the ELN.

In April 1967, Debray visited Guevara in a guerrilla camp in Ñancahuazú and offered to take up arms for the cause. Guevara nicknamed the pale, thin

---

"By reacting swiftly to newly captured information, you may be able to launch a successful operation against a guerrilla unit that only hours before seemingly could not be located."

—Felix Rodríguez

Communist scout Régis Debray (with mustache), speaking to the press in August 1967, was captured and roughed up by Bolivian soldiers. He told CIA operatives where they could find Guevara.

Frenchman Pan Blanco, or "White Bread." He did not think Debray would make much of a soldier. Rather than hiring him to fight, Guevara prepared a coded message for Debray to take to Castro. It was a request for desperately needed equipment, including field radios. Debray left the guerrilla camp on April 20 and was promptly captured by Bolivian forces upon entering the town of Muyupampa. Bolivian soldiers roughed him up before Rodríguez's operatives interrogated him exhaustively. The Frenchman willingly told the agents everything he knew about ELN operations. He provided information about soldiers, troop movements, and plans for future attacks. According to Rodríguez, "It was Debray's testimony . . . that helped convince the Agency [CIA] to lay on a concentrated effort to capture the elusive revolutionary [Guevara]. . . . [Debray's information] became our psychological road maps, giving us valuable clues about the people against whom we would operate."

WEAK **SOUP**

By then the ELN was close to collapse. Guevara's asthma had become crippling. He had no medicine to keep the asthma under control and had such difficulty breathing that he could not walk more than a few steps. He had to ride a mule for days at a time as he wheezed, vomited, coughed, and gasped for air. As Guevara wrote in his diary, "My asthma continues to wage war." The guerrillas spent most of their time looking for food. Some days they had nothing to eat but weak soup made from water and lard (animal fat). When the guerrillas approached local Indians to buy food, the Indians often fled or reported them to authorities. Rodríguez explained why the locals would not work cooperatively with the ELN:

> Bolivian Indians . . . do not customarily [grow] facial hair. So when they saw the Cuban guerrillas and their Peruvian and local Bolivian allies, all with beards and long hair, they were instinctively afraid and mistrustful of the outsiders. This oversight on the part of the guerrillas . . . made it harder for the Cubans to obtain supplies as they went from place to place.

Although dizzy, nauseous, and weak from starvation, the guerrillas managed to carry out a few successful attacks. In July they overran a small garrison in the town of Samaipata and captured a large supply of arms and ammunition. The revolutionaries also raided the town pharmacy in an unsuccessful search for asthma medicine for Che.

PREDICTING GUEVARA'S NEXT MOVE

The small victory at Samaipata was to be Che's last conquest. While Guevara never admitted that the mission was failing, his daily diary entries from August described the situation as distressing, desperate, and dreary. The monthly summary concluded, "We are at a low point in our morale and our revolutionary legend."

The last day of August spelled the beginning of the end for the ELN. Bolivian soldiers ambushed and slaughtered about ten ELN fighters. The single survivor, José Castillo Chávez, was a Bolivian. The soldiers turned him over to Rodríguez, who questioned him for several hours a day for more than two weeks.

Rodríguez considered Castillo Chávez to be an extremely valuable intelligence source and treated him well. Rather than beatings and deprivation, Rodríguez gave Castillo Chávez medical care, food, and tobacco. He lived in a comfortable locked room, not a cell. As Rodríguez

"THE WORST MONTH WE HAVE HAD"

Che Guevara kept a detailed diary of his Bolivian mission. In his "Summary of the Month" on the last day of August 1967, five weeks before his capture and execution, Guevara described the many problems that faced him and his men when Bolivian forces killed a small column of guerrillas, took prisoners, and captured important papers:

> Without doubt, this was the worst month we have had in this war. The loss of all . . . the documents and medicines was a heavy blow, psychologically above all else. The loss of two men at the end of last month and the subsequent march on only horsemeat [for food] demoralized the troops and sparked the first case of desertion. . . . The lack of contact with the outside . . . and the fact that the prisoners taken from this group talked [revealed secrets to their captors], also demoralized the troops somewhat. My illness sowed uncertainty among several others and all this was reflected in our only clash, one in which we should have inflicted several enemy casualties but only succeeded in wounding one of them. Besides this, the difficult march through the hills without water exposed some negative traits among the troops.

writes, "Torture or physical abuse of prisoners is totally counterproductive. The goal is to convert them to your point of view, not beat them into submission."

Castillo Chávez had not been particularly political before joining the ELN and was easy to convert. He said he was tricked into serving with the guerrillas with promises of an education in the Soviet Union and Cuba. When Castillo Chávez visited the ELN base camp, ready to travel abroad, he was instead ordered to fight. He received a knapsack, a canteen, a hammock, a rifle, and 120 rounds of ammunition.

Castillo Chávez provided Rodríguez with detailed information about the ELN, including its finances, field maneuvers, and names and nationalities of soldiers. This information allowed Rodríguez to predict exactly where Guevara would be moving next with his guerrilla force.

IN HOT PURSUIT

Acting on Rodríguez's intelligence, the Bolivian army was in hot pursuit. By the end of September, the ELN spent its days simply trying to avoid being caught. On September 28, Guevara wrote in his diary, "A day of anguish. At times it seemed as if it would be our last. . . . At 10 [in the morning] a group of 46 soldiers with their knapsacks passed by, taking ages to get out of sight. . . . 12:00 another group, this time 77 men, passed by. . . . Our refuge has no defense . . . and the possibilities of escape are remote."

By early October, Guevara's tattered army had dwindled to seventeen men as the Bolivian army closed in. Smelling victory, the various army units fell into a competition to see which one would capture the ultimate prize—

Guevara (third from the right) sits with Bolivian guerrillas a week before his death.

Guevara stands with his mule, Chico, in late September 1967.

the corpse of Che Guevara. With little water and food, the guerrillas moved from place to place, waiting for death. On October 7, the ELN took shelter in a forest high up a ravine. Guevara wrote the last entry in his Bolivian diary: "We have completed the 11th month of our guerrilla operation, [it] was spent in a bucolic [pleasant] mood, without complications."

The next day, a team of fresh, newly trained Bolivian rangers took positions on the steep walls above the guerrilla encampment. Other groups blocked the only exit from the ravine. If the guerrillas were to escape, they would have to fight their way out. After a tense standoff lasting several hours, Guevara's final battle erupted at 1:10 in the afternoon. The Bolivian soldiers rained a storm of mortar and machine gun fire down onto the guerrillas. Several ELN fighters were killed instantly. Guevara hid behind a rock and returned fire with his automatic rifle. A stray bullet smashed into the barrel of his gun, rendering it useless. Guevara was now unarmed. A bullet pierced his trademark beret, while a second shot slammed into his thigh. Guevara fell to the ground.

Bolivian army sergeant Bernardino Huanca came across Guevara lying in the brush. Huanca pointed his rifle at the world's most famous revolutionary hero. Che is said to have yelled out, "Don't shoot. I am Che Guevara. I am worth more to you alive than dead."

"Don't shoot. I am Che Guevara. I am worth more to you alive than dead."

—Che Guevara

"HE WAS A MESS"

Once a leader of revolution, Guevara was now a prisoner of the Bolivian army. He was locked in a small, mud-walled schoolhouse in the nearby village of La Higuera. Rodríguez heard the news of Guevara's capture on a field radio and notified the CIA in a long, coded message. The next day, October 9, Rodríguez flew to La Higuera, accompanied by a senior member of the Bolivian army, Colonel Joaquín Zenteno Anaya.

Rodríguez had official orders to keep Guevara alive at all costs. The CIA considered the revolutionary commander to be one of the most valuable intelligence sources ever captured. CIA helicopters and airplanes were standing by to transfer Guevara to Panama for interrogation. When Rodríguez finally met Guevara, he did not look like the revolutionary threat so many governments had feared for so long. Instead, "Che was lying on his side on the floor, his arms tied behind his back and his feet bound together. Near Che lay the corpses of two guerrillas. . . . Che's leg wound was slightly, but visibly, oozing blood. He was a mess. Hair matted, clothes ragged and torn," Rodríguez wrote.

Zenteno Anaya questioned Guevara, who refused to speak. In the colonel's absence, Rodríguez took a phone call with a message from Bolivia's president René Barrientos. It was a coded message to conduct operations 500 and 600. Operation 500 stood for Che Guevara. Operation 600 meant "kill."

The Bolivian plan was to execute Guevara but to tell the public that he had been killed in battle. If the international community knew that the guerrilla leader had been captured alive, some would demand that he be put on trial for his crimes. Barrientos wanted to avoid the worldwide attention a war trial would bring to Bolivia and its corrupt justice system. U.S. presidential adviser Walt Rostow listed another reason the Bolivians wanted Guevara dead. His execution would "have a strong impact in discouraging would-be guerrillas."

"SHOOT, COWARD!"

Rodríguez pleaded with Zenteno Anaya to ignore the kill order and to let Guevara live. The colonel responded, "If I don't comply with [follow] my orders to execute Che I will be disobeying my own president and I'll risk a dishonorable discharge [from the army]." It was eleven in the morning. Zenteno Anaya turned to leave. He told Rodríguez he would be back by two and wanted Guevara dead by that time. He did not care how the revolutionary was killed. "You can even do it yourself if you want, as I know how much harm he has brought your country [Cuba]."

At first, Rodríguez tried to come up with a plan to smuggle Guevara out of Bolivia alive. But he was on Bolivian soil and realized that he could

Felix Rodríguez (left) wanted to keep Guevara (center) alive, so he could be interrogated. But the Bolivian government wanted Guevara to be killed.

not ignore the president's orders. Rodríguez decided to have Guevara shot—but to make it look as if he was shot in battle, as the Bolivians wanted.

Once Rodríguez made the decision, he went back into the schoolhouse. He told Guevara that he had tried to prevent his execution and was sorry that he could not do so. Guevara told him it was all right and that he never should have been captured alive anyway. Guevara asked the CIA agent to tell his wife to remarry and try to be happy. Overcome with emotion, Rodríguez stepped forward and hugged his adversary. In his notes, Rodríguez wrote, "It was a tremendous emotional

THE ACCIDENTAL EXECUTIONER

Mario Terán, the man who fatally shot Che Guevara, was an accidental executioner. He was a low-level officer who happened to be near the Bolivian schoolhouse where Guevara was imprisoned. When another officer asked for a volunteer to kill Che, Terán raised his hand. Little is known about Terán's life before the event, but in the aftermath of the execution, he moved to Paraguay and assumed the alias Pedro Salazar. Some believe the CIA protected Terán for decades to safeguard him from Cuban assassins seeking revenge for Guevara's death. In 1996 biographer Jon Lee Anderson interviewed him and was not impressed:

Terán is a pathetic figure of a man who continues to live in hiding—at times wearing wigs and other disguises—out of fear for his life, convinced he has long been targeted for assassination by Cuba or its allies. Given a series of menial jobs by the army to keep him going, including that of bartender in the officers' club . . . Terán is a deeply bitter man, seeing himself as a scapegoat for his superior officers who have written books and gained glory and titles through their participation in Che's defeat.

moment for me. I no longer hated [Che]. His moment of truth had come, and he was conducting himself like a man, He was facing his death with courage and grace."

Mario Terán, a Bolivian sergeant, volunteered to shoot Guevara. He was eager to do so, as ELN guerrillas had recently killed three of his friends in battle. Rodríguez told Terán not to shoot Guevara in the head or face in typical execution style. Instead, he told him to aim anywhere from the neck down. That way, it would look as if Che had been killed in battle.

Terán was reportedly drunk—the soldiers had been drinking all night, celebrating Guevara's capture. A local peasant saw Terán approach the schoolhouse shouldering his semiautomatic rifle, carrying a beer in each hand. When Terán entered the building, he asked Guevara if he was thinking about his own death. Guevara said he was only thinking about the immortality of the revolution.

Terán shot the prisoner nine times, in the legs, chest, arm, shoulder, and throat. Che Guevara, revolutionary hero, was dead.

CHAPTER FIVE

THE MAKING OF AN ICON

> Your father has been a man who acted according to his beliefs and certainly has been faithful to his convictions.... [Try] always to be able to feel deeply any injustice committed against any person in any part of the world. It is the most beautiful quality of a revolutionary.
>
> —Che Guevara, in a 1965 letter to be read to his children after his death

On the afternoon of October 9, 1967, a stretcher holding Che Guevara's bloody body was strapped to the right landing skid of a helicopter. The chopper, with Rodríguez aboard, flew to Vallegrande, Bolivia, about 15 miles (25 km) from where Guevara had been killed. When the chopper landed, Rodríguez disappeared into the crowd. He did not want to be photographed or identified. Public exposure would ruin his career as a CIA agent. Che's body was loaded into an ambulance and taken to a hospital at Vallegrande, Nuestra Señora de Malta. The hospital's laundry room had become a temporary morgue to hold the remains of ELN guerrillas killed in battle the previous day.

Che's stretcher was placed atop a large concrete washbasin. Nuns working in the hospital brushed and trimmed his hair. A nurse, ordered by Bolivian officials to remove evidence of the fatal short-range rifle blasts, cleaned Guevara's wounds. To prevent the body from decomposing, a doctor injected formaldehyde into Guevara's neck. A parade of photographers, reporters, soldiers, and local citizens crowded around the body. With his brown eyes still open and his head propped up, Guevara looked to be at peace. Some thought he appeared to be still alive.

The Bolivian officers in charge of hunting down Guevara had good reason to display his remains to international reporters. They wanted the world to know, without any doubt, that the renowned Communist guerrilla

OPPOSITE: *Guevara's body was shown to the international press in Vallegrande, Bolivia.*

was dead. Che Guevara would never again foment revolution. However, the generals unwittingly helped create a lasting myth. Many of those gathered around Che's corpse had the feeling that Guevara strongly resembled Jesus, the main holy figure of Christianity. Several local women cut locks of his hair and kept them as blessings. One of those women later commented on Guevara's saintly appearance:

> *I was one of the first [at the hospital]. . . . What most amazed me was his expression, with his eyes open for eternity. . . . The whole experience affected me deeply. I was seeing a man who wanted good things for the world, who wanted justice, who dreamed of a better Latin America, of equality between men and women. And here they'd killed him.*

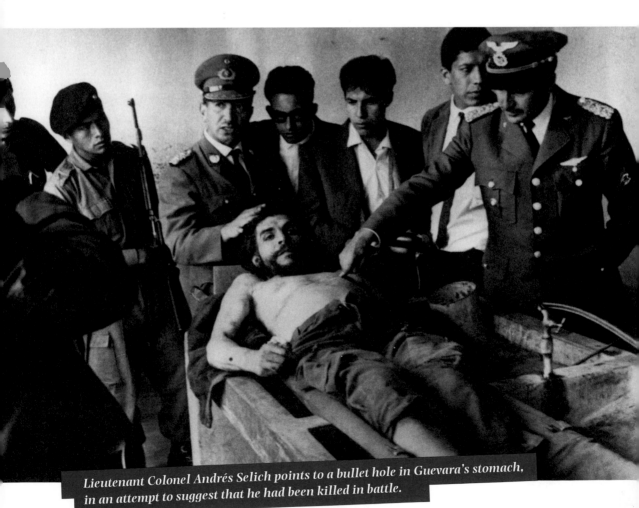

Lieutenant Colonel Andrés Selich points to a bullet hole in Guevara's stomach, in an attempt to suggest that he had been killed in battle.

BEYOND A REASONABLE DOUBT

As Guevara's body lay on the basin, Bolivian photographer Freddy Alborta took a photograph of the scene. The picture shows Bolivian officers standing around the corpse with soldiers and several local officials. A severed arm from another guerrilla lies on the floor. One of the officers, Lieutenant Colonel Andrés Selich, draws attention to the bullet wound in Guevara's stomach. The gesture was meant to seed the lie that Guevara had been killed in battle.

Like many others involved in the assassination, Selich kept a memento of the event—Guevara's leather briefcase. The executioner, Mario Terán, had taken the pipe Guevara puffed nearly constantly during the last years of his life. Rodríguez had taken Guevara's Rolex watch in La Higuera, immediately after the execution.

For even more undeniable, scientific proof that Che was dead and gone forever, General Alfredo Ovando Candía wanted to cut off Guevara's head and preserve it in a jar of formaldehyde. Rodríguez told him this was too barbaric and that a severed finger, with its fingerprint, would be enough proof. As a compromise, Ovando sawed off both Guevara's hands and preserved them in a jar. Experts compared the fingerprints to those on file in Argentina and confirmed Guevara's death.

As for Guevara's corpse, it was made to disappear. Before dawn on October 11, Selich and a few other officers dumped the body in a secret grave near the Vallegrande airstrip. A mass grave nearby was filled with the remains of the other ELN guerrillas killed in battle.

"LET THEM BE LIKE CHE"

On October 15, 1967, Fidel Castro acknowledged publically that Guevara had been assassinated and called for three days of pubic mourning in Cuba. On October 18, Castro gave a speech to more than one million solemn mourners gathered in Havana:

> If we wish to express what we want the people of future generations to be, we must say: Let them be like Che! If we wish to say how we want our children to be educated, we must say without hesitation: We want them to be educated in Che's spirit! If we want the model of a person, who does not belong to our time but to the future, I say from the depths of my heart that such a model, without

a single stain on his conduct, without a single stain on his action, without a single stain on his behavior, is Che! . . . Che has become a model for what future humans should be.

In the months that followed, millions of young people throughout the world took these words to heart. In 1968 protests erupted at college campuses and in big cities in Europe and the United States. The demonstrators demanded peace in Vietnam, an end to capitalist greed, and equality for all races. Some of them waved posters emblazoned with the famous 1960 photo of Che Guevara taken by Cuban photographer Alberto Korda. Many protesters expressed support for Communists in Cuba, North Vietnam, and the Congo. The demonstrators often clashed with police.

In the years to come, Che Guevara remained a powerful revolutionary icon in Africa, Latin America, and elsewhere. In the 1980s in Nicaragua, Communist revolutionaries displayed Guevara's picture prominently. Indian rebels used his image during an uprising in Mexico in the 1990s.

AN EPIC LIFE

Fidel Castro worked to keep Che Guevara's memory alive and to enhance his saintly image. In a 1971 speech, Castro praised Guevara as a noble man of the people, dedicated to revolution:

[Che] did not live for honors or glory. . . . Revolutionaries do not struggle for honor or glory, or to occupy a place in history. Che occupied, occupies, and will always occupy a great place in history because that was not important to him, because he was ready to die from the first battle on, because he was always absolutely selfless. And so his life became an epic, his life became an example.

SAINT ERNESTO OF LA HIGUERA

In 1997, on the thirtieth anniversary of Che Guevara's death, reporters from across the world traveled to Bolivia. They discovered that Guevara had been unofficially canonized, or declared a saint. Although church officials condemned this act, local Bolivians referred to the guerrilla warrior as San Ernesto de La Higuera, or Saint Ernesto of La Higuera. People in the region turned the hospital laundry where Guevara's corpse had been displayed into a shrine, or sacred place. They visited the shrine to offer prayers and ask favors from God. According to local legend, Guevara's ghost was often seen walking through the Bolivian ravines where he spent his last days.

In 2007, when the fortieth anniversary of Guevara's execution approached, reporters once again visited Bolivia. This time they found pictures of Guevara displayed in homes alongside images of key Christian figures—Jesus, the Virgin Mary, the pope, and Catholic saints.

The Bolivian hospital laundry where Che's body was taken has become a place of pilgrimage for people who view Guevara as a saint.

Stories of miracles performed by Saint Ernesto were numerous. A local woman, Primitiva Rojas, told a British reporter that she prayed to Guevara when she was very ill. She soon felt better. Rojas expressed her devotion: "I have lots of faith in him. Because he stopped existing does not mean he is not here with us. [After I prayed to Guevara], I dreamt of a man with a black beard and tender eyes, who was telling me: 'I was the one who cured you.'"

MERCHANDISING

Beyond Bolivia Guevara's memory remains alive on merchandise branded with the Korda photo. Che imagery has appeared in graffiti, on album covers, and in designer sunglasses ads. As reporter Isabel Hilton writes, Guevara's image "has been used to represent causes as diverse as world trade, anti-Americanism, teenage rebellion and Latin American identity. It has sold dolls, French wine, model cars, cigarette packets, stamps, Swatch

DIGGING UP CHE

In 1995 U.S. author Jon Lee Anderson was conducting research for his comprehensive biography of Che, *Che Guevara: A Revolutionary Life*. Anderson spoke to retired Bolivian general Mario Vargas Salinas, who told him that Guevara was buried near the airstrip in Vallegrande. This information sparked a search for Guevara's remains, which were finally discovered by a team of Cuban scientists in July 1997. Among seven bodies recovered near the airstrip, one man had amputated hands, indicating that the skeleton belonged to Guevara. The teeth in the skull perfectly matched those in a plaster mold of Guevara's teeth that had been made in Argentina. After the identification, the Cuban government flew the body to Cuba, along with the bodies of the other guerrillas buried nearby. Guevara was laid to rest with full military honors in a tomb in Santa Clara, site of his decisive 1958 victory against the Cuban army.

Benicio Del Toro (right) played Che Guevara in the 2008 Steven Soderbergh film Che.

watches, Austrian skis, ashtrays, mugs, key rings and nesting Russian dolls." In addition, Guevara has been a subject of paintings, sculptures, plays, and several popular movies. In *The Motorcycle Diaries* (2004), Gael García Bernal plays a young Che on his Latin American road trip with Alberto Granado. In *Che* (2008) Benicio Del Toro stars as Che the revolutionary. In 2009 Guevara became a character in a mobile phone video game, *El Che*.

A CONTRADICTION IN LIFE AND DEATH

Whatever his position in the marketplace, Che Guevara is also remembered because he personally challenged the CIA—the most powerful and secretive agency of the most powerful nation on earth. Many revere Guevara for treating the sick and standing up for the poor. But few care to discuss the brutality he exhibited as a guerrilla leader or his support of Fidel Castro, who imposed a harsh dictatorship on millions of Cuban people. In life Che Guevara was a political contradiction. In death he will always be young, brave, and defiant.

TIMELINE

1928   On June 14, Ernesto "Che" Guevara is born in Rosario, Argentina, to Ernesto Guevara Lynch Sr. and Celia de la Serna.

1931   Guevara is diagnosed with asthma.

1947   Guevara enrolls in medical school in Buenos Aires, Argentina.

1952   Between January and July, Guevara takes a six-month motorcycle journey with his friend Alberto Granado, visiting Argentina, Chile, Peru, Colombia, and Venezuela.

1953   Guevara graduates from medical school. He travels through South and Central America, arriving in Guatemala in December.

1955   While living in Mexico City, Mexico, Guevara meets Raúl and Fidel Castro, brothers planning a revolution in Cuba.

1956   On November 24, Guevara, the Castro brothers, and about eighty other men sail from Tuxpan, Mexico, to Cuba to launch the revolution there.

1957   Guevara establishes a revolutionary guerrilla base camp called El Hombrito, with a bakery, weapons workshop, shoemaking facility, and cigar production line.

1958   Rebel forces led by Guevara capture strategic locations around Santa Clara in central Cuba.

1959   On January 1, President Fulgencio Batista flees Cuba. The next day, Guevara, Castro, and their troops enter Havana to claim Cuba for the revolutionaries.

1960   As minister of industry, Guevara takes charge of Cuba's newly nationalized banks, factories, small businesses, and corporations. Guevara writes *Guerrilla Warfare: A Method* (published in 1963).

1961   An army of Cuban exiles trained by the U.S. Central Intelligence Agency (CIA) lands at the Bay of Pigs in a failed attempt to kill Castro and Guevara and to overthrow Cuba's revolutionary government.

1962   U.S. spy planes discover Soviet nuclear weapons in Cuba, setting off the Cuban Missile Crisis. The crisis is averted through top-secret negotiations between U.S. president John F. Kennedy and Soviet premier Nikita Khrushchev.

1963   Guevara publishes *Reminiscences of the Cuban Revolutionary War.*

1964   On December 11, Guevara gives a controversial and highly publicized speech titled "Colonialism Is Doomed" to the General Assembly of the United Nations in New York.

1965   Guevara disappears from public view, secretly traveling to the Congo in Africa to train guerrilla fighters to overthrow their repressive Western-backed government.

1966   Guevara flies to Bolivia to organize a guerrilla fighting force in the jungle to launch a revolution in this South American nation. The Bolivian military tracks Guevara.

1967   On October 9, Bolivian army sergeant Mario Terán executes Guevara on the orders of Bolivian president René Barrientos Ortuño.

1997   The remains of Che Guevara are exhumed next to an airfield in Vallegrande, Bolivia, flown to Cuba, and buried with full military honors in Santa Clara.

2004   The widely praised movie *The Motorcycle Diaries* opens in theaters. The story is based on journals Guevara kept during his travels through South America in 1952.

2008   Director Steven Soderbergh releases *Che,* a two-part film about Guevara that explores his revolutionary activities and his last days in the jungles of Bolivia.

2012   Luxury carmaker Mercedes-Benz displays a giant picture of Che Guevara (with a Mercedes logo on his beret) during a presentation about a car-sharing program designed to reduce automobile emissions.

GLOSSARY

capitalism: an economic system based on private property and free enterprise, with little government interference in business operations

Cold War: a period of intense hostility between the United States and the Soviet Union lasting from 1945 to the collapse of the Soviet Union in 1991

Communism: an economic system in which the central government controls all business activity, including employment, management, manufacturing, pricing, and sales

corporation: a privately owned, often very large company

counterrevolutionary: a person dedicated to overthrowing a government established by a previous revolution

coup d'état: the quick overthrow of a government, often by violence

dictator: a ruler who holds complete authority over a government and nation and often rules oppressively

exile: a person who leaves his or her home or country, usually because of a war or other major conflict that puts that person's life at risk

guerrillas: small groups of fighters who operate independently, using military practices such as sabotage, ambush, and bombings

intelligence: information about an enemy

interrogate: to formally question a prisoner or captive. Interrogation techniques vary from polite and well-ordered interviews to those based on violence and torture.

Latin America: all the Americas south of the United States, including Mexico, in which Spanish or Portuguese is the dominant language

Mafia: an organized, underground network that deals in illegal businesses such as gambling, narcotics, and prostitution

nationalize: to take over a private business and give control of its operations to the national government

Socialism: an economic system in which many, though not all, businesses are government owned and where a large portion of business profits go to provide services to citizens of the society

Soviet Union: a Communist nation of fifteen republics, with its capital in Moscow, Russia, that was created as a result of revolution in 1922 and collapsed in 1991

WHO'S WHO?

Jacobo Arbenz Guzmán (1913–1971) Arbenz was a Guatemalan military officer from 1944 to 1951, when he was elected president of Guatemala. A Socialist, Arbenz instituted a number of programs to lessen the widespread poverty in Guatemala. The United States opposed his attempt to nationalize 500,000 acres (200,000 hectares) of uncultivated land belonging to the U.S.-based United Fruit Company. After being ousted by a CIA-backed coup in 1954, Arbenz fled to Mexico City. He later lived in Paris, France; Prague, Czechoslovakia; and Moscow, Russia.

René Barrientos Ortuño (1919–1969) As a general, Barrientos took part in a 1952 Bolivian revolution, which toppled a repressive dictatorship. He was named commander of the Bolivian air force in 1952. Two years later, Barrientos became Bolivia's president, overthrowing the democratically elected president in a CIA-backed coup d'état. Barrientos personally ordered the execution of Che Guevara after he was captured in October 1967.

Fulgencio Batista (1901–1973) As Cuba's president, military leader, and dictator, Batista controlled the country from 1933 to 1944 and again from 1952 until 1959. Backed by the CIA and the U.S. Mafia, Batista led a corrupt and repressive regime that silenced political opposition with beatings, torture, and public executions. During his years as Cuba's leader, the police and the military killed an estimated twenty thousand Cubans. After the Cuban revolution of 1959, Batista fled his homeland and was eventually accepted by Portugal, where he died following a heart attack at the age of seventy-two.

Fidel Castro (1926–) Castro, a former lawyer, became a guerrilla leader in the mid-1950s. He was the leading force behind the Cuban revolution, which transformed the country into a Communist dictatorship in 1959. Castro served as dictator, prime minister, and president until 2006, when, due to ill health, he transferred power to his brother Raúl. During his long years in power, Fidel Castro developed a repressive secret police force that kept tight control over the Cuban media, educational system, and the lives of average citizens.

Raúl Castro (1931–) Raúl, Fidel Castro's brother, was a rebel commander in the 1950s, helping to lead the guerrilla armies that overthrew Fulgencio Batista in Cuba in 1959. After the revolution, Castro held a variety of positions, including the first vice president of the Cuban Council of State and minister of the Revolutionary Armed Forces. He resigned the latter post in 2006 to assume presidential duties when Fidel stepped down due to poor health.

Régis Debray (1940–) Originally from France, Debray was a crucial link for transferring money and communications between Fidel Castro in Cuba and Che Guevara's guerrillas in Bolivia in 1966 and 1967. Debray was arrested by Bolivian military authorities on April 20, 1967, and subjected to intense interrogation. He provided important information to authorities concerning the whereabouts of Guevara. Sentenced to thirty years in a Bolivian prison for his role in Guevara's guerrilla war, he was freed in 1970 after an international campaign for his release.

Hilda Gadea (1924–1974) A Peruvian economist and revolutionary of mixed Indian and Chinese heritage, Gadea was responsible for introducing Che Guevara to Cuban revolutionaries in Guatemala, where she was a political exile. Gadea married Guevara in 1955. The couple had a daughter, Hilda Beatriz, in 1956. They divorced in 1959. Gadea wrote the memoir *My Life with Che* in 1972.

Ernesto "Che" Guevara (1928–1967) Born in Argentina, Guevara was a Marxist revolutionary who worked to liberate Latin America from American and European business interests and political influence. Guevara was second in command to Fidel Castro during the guerrilla operations that overthrew Cuba's dictator Fulgencio Batista in 1959. After the revolution, Che served in a number of government positions, including judge, minister of industry, president of the national bank, and director of the Cuban armed forces. During the last years of his life, Guevara traveled the world, attempting to spread Cuban Socialism to other nations. He was assassinated in Bolivia by CIA-backed forces at the age of thirty-nine.

Aleida March (1937–) Before joining the Cuban Revolution, March was a teacher in Las Villas, Cuba. She joined the July 26 Movement to support Fidel Castro and his guerrilla fighters. When pursued by police, she took refuge in Guevara's guerrilla camp. Known for her exceptional beauty, March soon became Guevara's lover and was by his side when he rode triumphantly into Havana in early 1959. The couple married several months later at La Cabaña Fortress and eventually had four children. In 2008 March wrote the book *Evocation* about her life with Che Guevara.

Felix Rodríguez (1941–) Rodríguez was a young Cuban exile in Miami, Florida, when the CIA recruited him to participate in the Bay of Pigs operation. After that invasion of Cuba failed, Rodríguez joined Operation 40, a group of CIA agents who carried out covert executions of political enemies in foreign countries. Intelligence gathered by Rodríguez in Bolivia in 1967 led to the capture of Che Guevara that year. In the following years, Rodríguez worked for the CIA in Vietnam and Nicaragua.

Mario Terán (ca. 1940–) Terán was a Bolivian army sergeant in 1967 when he volunteered to execute Che Guevara. Allegedly drunk at the time, Terán pumped nine bullets into Guevara and then took the Cuban guerrilla's pipe as a souvenir. In the aftermath of the execution, he moved to Paraguay and assumed the alias Pedro Salazar. Some say the CIA protected Terán for decades to safeguard him from Cuban assassins seeking revenge for Guevara's death.

SOURCE NOTES

5   Reuters, "Bolivia Confirms Guevara's Death; Body Displayed," *New York Times,* 2010, http://www.nytimes.com/learning/general/onthisday/big/1009.html (September 13, 2011).

5   Jon Lee Anderson, *Che Guevara: A Revolutionary Life* (New York: Grove Press, 1997), 739.

9   Ibid., 124.

9   Ernesto Guevara, *Young Che* (New York: Vintage Books, 2008), 53.

10   Ibid., 100.

11   Ibid., 107.

12   Ibid., 108–109.

13   Anderson, *Che Guevara,* 36.

13   Nick Caistor, *Che Guevara: A Life* (Northampton, MA: Interlink Books, 2010), 10–11.

13   Ibid., 11.

14   Ernesto Guevara, *The Motorcycle Diaries* (London: Harper Perennial, 2004), 68.

17   Caistor, *Che Guevara: A Life,* 20.

20   Anderson, *Che Guevara,* 126.

20   Ibid.

21   Ibid., 125.

25   Ernesto Guevara, *The Bolivian Diary* (New York: Ocean Press, 2006), 6.

25   Hilda Gadea, *My Life with Che: The Making of a Revolutionary* (New York: Palgrave Macmillan, 2008), 143.

26   Fidel Castro, *Che,* ed. David Deutschmann (Melbourne: Ocean Press, 1994), 99.

26   Jorge G. Castañeda, *Compañero: The Life and Death of Che Guevara* (New York: Alfred A. Knopf, 1997), 95.

27   Michael Ratner and Michael Steven Smith, eds., *Che Guevara and the FBI* (Melbourne: Ocean Press, 1997), 15.

28   Herbert L. Matthews, *Fidel Castro* (New York: Simon and Schuster, 1969), 109.

29   Ernesto Guevara, *Episodes of the Cuban Revolutionary War,* 1956–58 (New York: Pathfinder, 1996), 151.

30   Che Guevara, "Guerrilla Warfare: A Method," *Marxist Internet Archive,* 2005, http://www.marxists.org/archive/guevara/1963/09/guerrilla-warfare.htm (January 6, 2012).

31   Ernesto Guevara, *Episodes of the Cuban Revolutionary War,* 235.

32   Ratner and Smith, *Che Guevara and the FBI,* 20.

32   Ibid., 26.

34   Castañeda, *Compañero,* 132.

34   Caistor, *Che Guevara: A Life,* 62.

35   Ibid., 63.

37   Ibid., 64.

39   Anderson, *Che Guevara,* 396.

39   Castañeda, *Compañero,* 141.

41   Anderson, *Che Guevara,* 386.

42   Saul Landau, "After Castro," *Mother Jones*, July–August 1989, 26.

43   Anderson, *Che Guevara,* 395.

43   Ibid., 421.

48   Ibid., 609.

49   Homer Bigart, "Bazooka Fired at U.N. as Cuban Speaks," *New York Times,* December 12, 1964, n.d., http://www.latinamericanstudies.org/belligerence/bazooka.htm (January 6, 2012).

50   Che Guevara, "At the United Nations," *Marxist Internet Archive,* 2005, http://www.marxists.org/archive/guevara/1964/12/11.htm (January 6, 2012).

50   Anderson, *Che Guevara,* 629.

52   Guevara, *The Bolivian Diary,* 253.

55   Castañeda, *Compañero,* 335.

55   Ibid., 370.

58   Felix I. Rodríguez and John Weisman, *Shadow Warrior* (New York: Simon and Schuster, 1989), 130–131.

59   Castañeda, *Compañero,* 136.

60   Guevara, *The Bolivian Diary,* 185.

60   Rodríguez and Weisman, *Shadow Warrior,* 135.

60   Guevara, *The Bolivian Diary,* 222.

61   Ibid., 221–222.

61   Ibid., 148.

62   Ernesto Guevara, *The Complete Bolivian Diaries of Che Guevara and Other Captured Documents,* ed. James Daniel (New York: Cooper Square Press, 2000), 218.

63   Ibid., 222.

64   Anderson, *Che Guevara,* 733.

64   Rodríguez and Weisman, *Shadow Warrior,* 162.

65   Peter Kornbluh, "White House Memorandum, October 11, 1967," *National Security Archive,* November 1997, http://www.gwu.edu/~nsarchiv/NSAEBB/NSAEBB5/che7_1.htm (January 6, 2012).

65   Rodríguez and Weisman, *Shadow Warrior,* 164.

65   Ibid.

66   Anderson, *Che Guevara,* 750.

66–67   Ibid., 739.

69   Ibid., 634.

70   Michael Casey, *Che's Afterlife* (New York: Vintage Books, 2009), 179.

71–72   Castro, *Che,* 78.

72   Ibid., 99.

74   Andres Schipani, "The Final Triumph of Che," *Guardian,* September 23, 2007, http://www.guardian.co.uk/world/2007/sep/23/theobserver.worldnews (September 13, 2011).

74–75   Isabel Hilton, "Still a Messiah?" *New Statesman,* October 4, 2007, http://www.newstatesman.com/politics/2007/10/che-guevara-image-revolution (September 13, 2011).

SELECTED BIBLIOGRAPHY

Anderson, Jon Lee. *Che Guevara: A Revolutionary Life*. New York: Grove Press, 1997.

Bigart, Homer. "Bazooka Fired at U.N. as Cuban Speaks." *New York Times,* December 12, 1964. N.d. http://www.latinamericanstudies.org/belligerence/bazooka.htm (January 17, 2011).

Caistor, Nick. *Che Guevara: A Life*. Northampton, MA: Interlink Books, 2010.

Casey, Michael. *Che's Afterlife*. New York: Vintage Books, 2009.

Castañeda, Jorge G. *Compañero: The Life and Death of Che Guevara*. New York: Alfred A. Knopf, 1997.

Castro, Fidel. *Che*. Edited by David Deutschmann. Melbourne: Ocean Press, 1994.

DeCosse, Sarah A. "Cuba's Repressive Machinery." *Human Rights Watch*. 1999. http://www.hrw .org/legacy/reports/1999/cuba/index.htm#TopOfPage (September 13, 2011).

Gadea, Hilda. *My Life with Che: The Making of a Revolutionary*. New York: Palgrave Macmillan, 2008.

Glüsing, Jens. "The Curse of Che Guevara." *Spiegel,* November 8, 2007. http://www.spiegel.de /international/world/0,1518,druck-510155,00.html (September 13, 2011).

Guevara, Ernesto. "At the United Nations." *Marxist Internet Archive*. 2005. http://www.marxists .org/archive/guevara/1964/12/11.htm (September 13, 2011).

———. *The Bolivian Diary*. New York: Ocean Press, 2006.

———. *The Complete Bolivian Diaries of Che Guevara and Other Captured Documents*. Edited by James Daniel. New York: Cooper Square Press, 2000.

———. *Episodes of the Cuban Revolutionary War, 1956–58*. New York: Pathfinder, 1996.

———. *The Motorcycle Diaries*. London: Harper Perennial, 2004.

———. *Young Che*. New York: Vintage Books, 2008.

Hilton, Isabel. "Still a Messiah?" *New Statesman,* October 4, 2007. http://www.newstatesman .com/politics/2007/10/che-guevara-image-revolution (September 13, 2011).

Kornbluh, Peter. "The Death of Che Guevara: Declassified." *National Security Archive*. 1997. http:// www.gwu.edu/~nsarchiv/NSAEBB/NSAEBB5 (September 13, 2011).

———. "White House Memorandum, October 11, 1967." *National Security Archive*. November 1997. http://www.gwu.edu/~nsarchiv/NSAEBB/NSAEBB5/che7_1.htm (September 13, 2011).

Matthews, Herbert L. *Fidel Castro*. New York: Simon and Schuster, 1969.

Ratner, Michael, and Michael Steven Smith, eds. *Che Guevara and the FBI*. Melbourne: Ocean Press, 1997.

Reuters. "Bolivia Confirms Guevara's Death; Body Displayed." *New York Times*. 2010. http://www .nytimes.com/learning/general/onthisday/big/1009.html (September 13, 2011).

Rodriguez Felix I., and John Weisman. *Shadow Warrior*. New York: Simon and Schuster, 1989.

Russell, Dick. *The Man Who Knew Too Much*. New York: Carroll & Graf, 1992.

Schipani, Andres. "The Final Triumph of Che." *Guardian,* September 23, 2007. http://www .guardian.co.uk/world/2007/sep/23/theobserver.worldnews (September 13, 2011).

Villegas, Harry. *Pombo: A Man of Che's Guerrilla*. New York: Pathfinder, 1997.

FURTHER READING, FILMS, AND WEBSITES

BOOKS

Abrams, Dennis. *Ernesto "Che" Guevara.* New York: Chelsea House, 2010.
Part of the Great Hispanic Heritage series, this book provides detailed biographical information about Guevara, from his childhood in Argentina to his death in Bolivia.

Boyle, David. *Understanding the Communist Manifesto.* New York: Rosen Publishing Group, 2010.
The Communist Manifesto (1848) by Karl Marx and Friedrich Engels is one of the world's most influential political documents and one that inspired Che Guevara to lead a revolution. This volume discusses why the document was written, how it was received, and its ongoing impact on societies around the world.

Campbell, Kumari. *Cuba in Pictures.* Minneapolis: Twenty-First Century Books, 2004.
This book explores Cuba from many angles: geographical, historical, political, and cultural. The text includes an examination of Cuba's revolution and its lasting impact on Cuban society.

Di Piazza, Francesca Davis. *Bolivia in Pictures.* Minneapolis: Twenty-First Century Books, 2008.
The book explores the geographic, historical, economic, and cultural landscapes of Bolivia, the South American nation where Guevara spent his last days.

Havelin, Kate. *Che Guevara.* Minneapolis: Twenty-First Century Books, 2007.
This biography gives a thorough overview of Che Guevara's life and includes photos of him in the field and as a family man.

Lankford, Ronnie D., ed. *Is Socialism Harmful?* Detroit: Greenhaven Press, 2011.
This book contains articles written by scholars, politicians, and other experts who debate the pros and cons of Socialism.

Markel, Rita J. *Fidel Castro's Cuba.* Minneapolis: Twenty-First Century Books, 2007.
Part of the Dictatorships series, this book examines the life of Fidel Castro, how and why he came to power in Cuba, and the workings of his dictatorial government.

Prentzas, G. S. *The Cuban Revolution.* New York: Chelsea House, 2011.
This book looks at the five decades in which Cuba has functioned as a one-party Socialist state. It includes an examination of U.S. relations with Cuba and the difficult economic conditions endured by Cuba's citizens.

FILMS

Che. DVD. Directed by Steven Soderbergh. 2008. New York: Criterion Collection, 2010.
This two-part film stars Benicio Del Toro as Che Guevara. Part 1 dramatizes Guevara's work with the Cuban revolution. Part 2 examines his struggles in the Bolivian jungle.

The Motorcycle Diaries. DVD. Directed by Walter Salles. 2004. Hollywood, CA: Universal Studios, 2009.
Gael García Bernal stars as young Che Guevara, who sets off on a motorcycle trip through Latin America with his friend Alberto Granado. Already aware of the plight of the poor, Guevara further awakens to the injustices of the capitalist system on this journey.

WEBSITES

CIA: 1947–1990
http://www.spartacus.schoolnet.co.uk/2WWcia.htm
This page features an extensive history of the U.S. Central Intelligence Agency, from its founding after World War II (1939–1945) through the postwar decades when the agency worked to fight Communism around the world. Links take readers to information about specific CIA operations and operatives in Cuba, Guatemala, and elsewhere in Latin America.

Ernesto Che Guevara Texts
http://chehasta.narod.ru/cheguevaraeng.htm
This site features letters, speeches, diary entries, and other texts written by Che Guevara between 1958 and 1967. Included are his manuals on guerrilla warfare and his historic 1964 speech to the United Nations.

Library of Economic Liberties: Marxism
http://www.econlib.org/library/Enc/Marxism.html
This site contains essays by more than 150 top economists. The writings explain economic and political systems studied by Che Guevara, including Communism and capitalism.

National Security Archive
http://www.gwu.edu/~nsarchiv
This website, run by George Washington University, publishes political documents on a wide range of topics. The Latin American section features CIA reports about activities in Guatemala, Cuba, and other Latin American nations, with extensive reporting on Che Guevara.

INDEX

ABOUT THE AUTHOR

Stuart A. Kallen has written more than 250 nonfiction books for children and young adults over the past twenty years. His books have covered a wide arc of human history, culture, and science, from the building of the pyramids in Egypt to the music of the twenty-first century. Some of his recent titles include *The Aftermath of the Sandinista Revolution; Open the Jail Doors—We Want to Enter: The Defiance Campaign against Apartheid Laws, South Africa, 1952; We Are Not Beasts of Burden: Cesar Chavez and the Delano Grape Strike, California, 1965–1970; Postmodern Art;* and *The History of Rock and Roll.* Kallen, who lives in San Diego, California, is also a singer-songwriter and guitarist.

PHOTO ACKNOWLEDGMENTS

The images in this book are used with the permission of: © TNT Magazine/Alamy, p. 4; © Keystone-France/Gamma Keystone via Getty Images, pp. 5, 43, 62; © Interfoto/Personalities/Alamy, p. 6; © Apic/Hutlon Archive/Getty Images, pp. 8, 11, 12, 27; © Emiliano Rodriguez/Alamy, p. 14; © Eliot Elisofon/Time & Life Pictures/Getty Images, p. 16; © Frank Scherschel/Time & Life Pictures/Getty Images, p. 18; © Grey Villet/Time & Life Pictures/Getty Images, p. 21; © Leonard Mccombe/Time Life Pictures/Getty Images, pp. 22–23; © Joseph Scherschel/Time & Life Pictures/Getty Images, p. 24; © Lee Lockwood/Time & Life/Getty Images, p. 29; © Transcendental Graphics/Archive Photos/Getty Images, p. 31; Enrique Meneses/Rex USA/Courtesy Everett Collection, p. 34; AP Photo, pp. 35, 47, 68; © Burt Glinn/Magnum Photos, pp. 36–37; Alberto Korda/AFP/Getty Images/Newscom, p. 38; © Keystone/Hulton Archives/Getty Images, p. 40; © Graf/Stringer/Hulton Archives/Getty Images, p. 46; © Bettmann/CORBIS, pp. 49, 56, 59, 63, 70; © Salas Archive Photos/Alamy, p. 52; Agence France Presse/Newscom, p. 54; AP Photo/Courtesy of Felix Rodriguez, p. 65; © Ira Block/National Geographic Society/CORBIS, p. 73; © Wild Bunch/Morena Films/Kobal Collection/Art Resource, NY, p. 75.

Front cover: © Joseph Scherschel/Time Life Pictures/Getty Images.

Main body text set in Conduit ITC Std 12/15.
Typeface provided by International Typeface Corp.